IN

John Douglas ACI
Alexander Shaw BAINES (70) Herbert BAMFORD (72)
Christopher James BULMER (11)
Jack Leo COXON (76) Leo Anthony COXON (44)
David James CRABTREE (30) Harry CRABTREE (76)
Derek DEMPSEY (46)
Muriel FIRTH (56) Samuel FIRTH (86)
Andrew FLETCHER (11) Edmond FLETCHER (63)
John FLETCHER (34) Peter FLETCHER (32)
Nellie FOSTER (64)
Felix Winspear GREENWOOD (13) Peter GREENWOOD (46)
Rupert Benedict GREENWOOD (11)
Norman HALL (71) Peter Anthony HALLIDAY (34)
Arthur HARTLEY (79)
Edith HINDLE (79) Frederick HINDLE (76)
Moira Helen HODGSON (15) Eric HUDSON (72)
John HUGHES (64) John HUTTON (74)
Walter KERR (76) Peter Charles LOVELL (43)
Jack LUDLAM (55)
Gordon Stuart McPHERSON (39) Irene McPHERSON (28)
Roy MASON (74) Frederick Norman MIDDLETON (84)
Harold MITCHELL (79) Elizabeth MUHL (21)
Ernest NORMINGTON (74)
Gerald Priestley ORMONDROYD (40) Richard John ORMONDROYD (12)
Robert Ian ORMONDROYD (12)
Sylvia Lund POLLARD (69) Herbert PRICE (78)
Amanda Jane ROBERTS (20) Jayne SAMPSON (18)
William STACEY (72)
Craig Albert STOCKMAN (14) Jane Ashley STOCKMAN (16)
Trevor John STOCKMAN (38)
Howard Malcolm TURNER (41) Sarah Elizabeth TURNER (16)
Simon Neil WARD (18) Robert WEDGEWORTH (72)
William James WEST (78) Adrian Mark WRIGHT (11)

Four Minutes To Hell

The Story of the Bradford City Fire

Paul Firth

WITH A FOREWORD BY TERRY YORATH

The Parrs Wood Press
MANCHESTER

First Published 2005

THE PARRS WOOD PRESS
St Wilfrid's Enterprise Centre
Royce Road, Manchester, M15 5BJ
www.parrswoodpress.com

ISBN: 1 903158 73 7

Printed by Newton Printing Ltd of London
www.newtonprinting.com

ACKNOWLEDGEMENTS

The extracts from the Moelwyn Hughes Report (Cmnd 6846) into the 1946 Burnden Park disaster, from the Wheatley Report (Cmnd 4952) into the 1971 Ibrox disaster and from the Popplewell Report (Cmnd 9585) into the 1985 deaths at Bradford and Birmingham are Crown Copyright. The citation from the Supplement to the *London Gazette* of 28th May 1986 is also Crown Copyright. Crown copyright material is reproduced with the permission of the Controller of HMSO and the Queen's Printer for Scotland.

The extract from *The Beautiful Game? Searching for the soul of football* by David Conn, published by Yellow Jersey, is reprinted by permission of the Random House Group Ltd.

The extracts from *Benchmark: Life, Laughter and the Law* by Sir Oliver Popplewell, published by I.B.Tauris and Co Ltd, are reprinted by kind permission of Sir Oliver Popplewell.

I would also like to thank a number of people without whom this book would never have been written. Alison and John at Special Collections, The J.B. Priestley Library, University of Bradford, have given every possible assistance with the Inquiry papers and have put up with me and my talking. All of those who gave of their time and emotions in interviews were absolutely indispensable to me. Their names will be obvious during the course of the book. How some of them managed to speak to me about something so personal, I shall never know. Some went on to encourage and help me further, especially when I needed that encouragement. Most of all I have enjoyed the immense support and bright ideas of Ann and David, my wife and son. Thank you all.

Photographs have been reproduced by kind permission of bantamspast.co.uk., Yorkshire Post Newspapers, the Controller of HMSO and Queen's Printer for Scotland, Peter Bell and the Bradford Telegraph & Argus.

FOREWORD

by Terry Yorath

Twenty years on, the Bradford fire is still very fresh in my mind. Any time I smell smoke or see flames, or even when someone starts talking about that dreadful day, it all comes back to me: it's an immediate reminder of what happened. The title of this book sums up what it was like for everyone involved. I can recall the fire starting, trying to get people out, making sure my family were alright and then managing to escape myself. I'll never forget the heat, the black smoke, the utter confusion and the fact that 56 people were burnt to death after going to watch a game of football.

Bradford City will always be very dear to me because I began my managerial career at Valley Parade, but the fire forged a special bond between everyone at the club at that time. I don't remember the names of all the players I've been in charge of over the last 20 years but I can recall everything about that squad. I remember the type of people they were, their characteristics and even their individual habits.

The day after the fire, I was interviewed on local TV and I said that a tragedy like that put everything in perspective. It didn't matter about the stand or where we were going to play next season - football wasn't important - but you only had to visit the injured in hospital - as all the players did - to realise that Bradford City meant an awful lot to our supporters. A few days later, Stuart McCall took the championship trophy to the special burns unit at Pinderfields Hospital in Wakefield to show his father, Andy, who'd been badly burned in the fire. Stuart was worried that it might seem a little insensitive, but the visit actually united the victims and reminded them of the reason they'd been at Valley Parade on that awful day. We got the same reaction in whichever hospital ward we went to. The fans, with bandages wrapped around their heads and hands, would congratulate us on our successful season and say they'd be supporting us again in August. It was extraordinary to hear them being so positive about something so very negative.

Once the final death toll had been arrived at, there was a stream of funerals - up to eight a week - and the players were magnificent. If the manager, Trevor Cherry, or I couldn't attend, we would delegate a couple of them instead, but they had to go in pairs because we didn't want them going on their own - we weren't sure how they'd cope. Not one of them said they didn't think they could do it but if they had, of course, we wouldn't have insisted. They all stuck together and carried out their tasks on a rota basis - they were brilliant.

Of course, nothing can compare with the terrible loss of life and suffering but as I look back on the fire, I do feel for the players. During my career, I've been fortunate enough to play for and manage my country in some very important matches. I've appeared in FA Cup and European Cup finals and I think it's sad that the members of that Bradford City squad will always be remembered for something completely different that happened on the day when they should have been celebrating a hugely important achievement in their careers.

11th May 1985 will remain one of the darkest dates in the history of British football but, thankfully, some good has come out of such an appalling tragedy. Post-Bradford, Heysel and Hillsborough, our grounds are now much safer. We must never forget those devastating four minutes at Valley Parade - I know I never will - and I'm pleased to be able to contribute these few words to a book that maintains the memory of those who died or were injured in the Bradford fire.

ONE

For years past I had wanted to write something about the fire at Valley Parade on 11th May 1985, but, like so many others who have to hold down the day job, I never quite managed to get round to it. And then I realised that the twentieth anniversary of the fire was almost upon us and there were many people interested in football, including even a number of Bradford City supporters, who knew little or nothing of what happened that day. Twenty years on, the fans had quite naturally changed as the club had gone through the most dramatic upheavals. So many of those fans weren't even born twenty years ago. Word of mouth was the only way any account of the events was being passed down and some of that was haphazard and possibly unreliable.

Unlike other disasters, it didn't make the national news each year. We carried on with our annual service of remembrance, even if fewer and fewer seemed to turn up. We had our memorials - the bas relief higher up the new stand than it had once been, the names of those who died cut in marble by the main entrance to the ground and the sculpture in Centenary Square, right in the middle of the city, which has always been my special memorial. But I thought we were beginning to forget. Worse still, we weren't leaving a proper record for the future.

My fear was reinforced by two events. We'd always had a minute's silence at the last home game of the season. Maybe we were having a minute's silence on too many occasions, but one year, from memory it was probably 2001 or 2002, we didn't remember our own dead. An enquiry with the club brought a rather distasteful reply on behalf of the then chairman to the effect that it was time to move on. Some of us wondered if the truth was that somebody had just forgotten and hadn't been prepared to admit it. Or maybe someone really did think that those of us who turned up to games regularly and especially those who had climbed out of that stand on that day should, at least officially, forget how lucky we were.

Then, sometime during 2004, I bought a book called *The Beautiful Game?*, written by David Conn. The book is essentially about how football and its finances are managed and it's a good read for any fan interested in the game and how its finances have come close to ruining clubs. Bradford City at the turn of the millennium provides an excellent case history for the mismanagement of football finances and so it is no surprise that a whole chapter is devoted to the club's "Six weeks of madness". The chapter begins, however, on Sunday morning 11th May 2003, the 18th anniversary of the fire. The author describes the ceremony and then says, "Largely unnoticed by the nation, they have been performing this annual service for eighteen years. The fire at Bradford City's Valley Parade ground in May 1985 is somehow football's less-remembered disaster." Maybe that sentence just confirmed my fears. It certainly gave me a fresh incentive.

Later I came across another book, which just set me thinking in a very different direction, that after all I should simply allow the events of that day to be quietly set aside by all save those most closely involved. This second book was actually recommended to me by its author, Sir Oliver Popplewell. If the author can't recommend his book, who can? As Mr Justice Popplewell, he had conducted the public inquiry into the fire. In his book, *Benchmark*, published in 2003, he recalled his memories of those Bradfordians with whom he came into contact. He was able to use the looking-glass of history to make a contrast with different reactions to more recent events. He wrote "Comparing the reaction of those involved in the Bradford disaster with those involved in some other disasters, one can only be astonished at the wonderful way that the citizens of Bradford behaved. They quietly buried their dead, tended their injured and comforted their bereaved. Not for them the noisy and public whingeing and whining which has been the hallmark of so many other disasters. They did not pursue seemingly endless inquiries as a personal vendetta. They did not seek to use their disaster as a weapon of emotional blackmail on the government, not (sic) did they seek to perpetuate publicly the memory of the terrible disaster they had suffered. They behaved with great dignity and no little courage. It is sad that the example so bravely set by Bradford was not followed by others."

When I first read that passage, my immediate reaction was one of pride. We Yorkshiremen are, I suppose, known to be rather dour, even to the point of stoicism. We don't cry, at least not in public, and we don't easily make a song and dance of essentially private matters. We traditionally keep ourselves very much to ourselves. I was indeed proud to see that a High Court judge felt able to describe that as "great dignity". But when I had time to think about what Sir Oliver had written, once more I found myself in a dilemma. By asking questions about the day, recording the answers, writing them down and then trying to have all that reproduced so that anyone could read about the public and private horrors of that day, wasn't I just going in the very opposite direction to that taken by my fellow citizens and so much admired by Sir Oliver? Wasn't I seeking "to perpetuate publicly the memory of the terrible disaster they had suffered"?

I suspected that I was doing just that and so I wondered if my writing it all down could be justified for other reasons. Soon I was given plenty of reason to continue. Once I started to ask questions, I was given the names of other people I should speak to. As I asked more questions, I came across some truly heroic deeds and I found some incredible modesty. Even though it necessitated making public some considerable distress, the importance of making equally public the "great dignity and no little courage" was enough in my eyes to justify my carrying on.

Then I found a silver lining in a rather unforeseen cloud. Because of an unexpected illness I was unable to continue with my normal work over a period of some months. I needed some therapy, something to occupy my brain. I thought I'd see if I could find enough material to form the basis for a book or at least some form of record of the disaster. I wanted it remembering for many more years to come. Even then it occurred to me that maybe others wanted to forget. So I spoke to those most likely to want to forget. I already knew someone who had lost her father that day. I knew fans who had escaped with differing degrees of injuries. I knew I could find police officers and players who had been there. Each person I spoke to was given the same choice at the very outset; if you don't want to talk to me - and most of the time I was talking to total strangers - I'll understand. After all, there had been plenty of times when I hadn't wanted to talk about the fire, let alone talk in a very public fashion about it.

Hardly anyone I approached turned me down. Even those who had suffered the most gave of their time and went through every conceivable emotion as they recalled their own personal tragedies. It seemed to me that these people, the ones who had most right to say that the day should be quietly put to the back of our minds and remembered only privately by those who had suffered most, these people in particular wanted to have May 11th remembered. They inspired me to carry on with my researches and to tell their stories. No one can tell the whole story of that day, because there are too many people with too many memories, some of whom I'm sure wouldn't have wanted to discuss them. And so I've tried to tell as much of the story as I can through the eyes of just a few of those who were there, some of whom saved lives, some of whom were themselves saved and some of whom lost family and friends. In one way or another all of them were injured. Most of them carry those injuries to this day, some more lightly than others.

What follows, then, is their story. It comes from just a small number of those who were there. I hope many others who were there or were directly affected by the fire will recognise the stories I've tried to tell. More than that, I hope those who don't know what happened will take a little time to find out more and then perhaps understand why some of us still want to have that day remembered with dignity for a long time yet.

TWO

On 9th March 1946 33 people died at a football match in Bolton after a wall collapsed. Bolton's previous highest crowd that season had been 43,000. Some 50,000 were expected that day. It is estimated that nearer to 85,000 squeezed into the ground. There was an inquiry into the causes of the disaster at Burnden Park. Recommendations were inevitably made to prevent any recurrence of the events that resulted in the deaths of those people. The most important of those recommendations was that football grounds should be licensed by the Local Authority. The inquiry recommended that, "The issue of the licence would depend upon satisfying the authority as to the construction and equipment of the ground, its compliance with regulations and the proposed maximum figures of admission to the different parts." So Burnden Park couldn't happen again, could it?

I suppose if you want to be especially pedantic, you can say that there has been no exact repetition of what happened back in 1946. But the disasters at Ibrox in 1971 and at Hillsborough in 1989 have some remarkable similarities to Burnden Park. Like Bolton, both involved crushing as a cause of death - too many people in too small a space. Particularly in relation to Hillsborough that phrase from the 1946 Moelwyn Hughes report, "the proposed maximum figures of admission to the different parts", strikes a truly tragic chord. Very probably back in 1946 no one thought that "the different parts" of a football ground meant much more than the four sides of the ground. Perhaps some grounds had one or more sides with seating and standing areas next to each other, different parts in that sense. Certainly no one thought then that grounds would be divided up into pens, either to keep the opposing armies of hooligans apart or at least to contain them within manageable areas. For that is exactly what had happened at Hillsborough by 1989. It was too simple, to the point of distortion, to say that there were too many people in the Leppings Lane end of the ground. The ticket allocation was calculated on the basis that there was sufficient room for the Liverpool fans. After all there had been no one crushed to death at the same ground when the previous year's cup semi-final had been played there.

"The different parts" of the Leppings Lane end were different pens and, while there were "proposed maximum figures of admission" to each pen in the eyes of Sheffield Wednesday Football Club, these figures were the club's own, were probably too high and there were no such figures as far as the City Council and its safety certificate were concerned. Indeed the Leppings Lane end been altered and divided into pens since the most recent certificate had been issued almost ten years before the 1989 deaths. Worst of all, there was no way of calculating with any accuracy how many spectators were in each pen. One of the other recommendations from the 1946 Burnden Park enquiry was that clubs should have a mechanical means of counting those entering the ground. The absence of the clicking turnstile at least explains all those crowd figures in the early part of the twentieth century where the attendance is so frequently expressed as a round number. Long before 1989 all Football League clubs counted their attendances by means of clicking turnstiles. Sheffield Wednesday - and they were almost certainly not alone here - did not arrange matters so that each turnstile could lead only to one "part" of the ground, to one pen.

As if to prove further that football is not especially good at learning from the history of its own disasters, there is another irony about that safety certificate for Hillsborough. When in early 1986 Mr Justice Popplewell wrote his final report into the fire at Bradford City and the disorder at Birmingham City, among other recommendations he suggested an annual renewal of the certificate, a duty on the local authority to inspect the premises prior to re-issuing the certificate and the power to revoke instead of merely to vary a certificate. Part of his reasoning behind this recommendation was expressed in these words: "It would ensure that there is an annual inspection; secondly it would give the local authority added power if a club were dragging its feet in carrying out some work which is required by the local authority." Perhaps, with his wish to hold an annual inspection, he had in mind the need to take into account significant alterations to the construction of the grounds and the use to which they were to be put. Sheffield City Council would surely have seen and acted upon the changes to the Leppings Lane end, if only there had been an annual inspection after the issue of the 1979 certificate.

One of the ironies about all this is that it is literally true that Burnden Park could not now happen again, despite the pessimism of the 1946 enquiry. The report acknowledged that "Compliance with the recommendations of this Report will cost money. They will involve grounds in a loss of gate money on popular days." The report went further and, in its most pessimistic tone, conceded that "It would be idle to suggest that the grounds, or large sections of them, should be rebuilt." While not actually rebuilding Burnden Park, Bolton Wanderers, one could say, went even further and moved to a new ground, built very much with the safety of its paying customers in mind. Many other clubs have substantially rebuilt their grounds and a few, like Bolton, have built new grounds. Safety at these redeveloped or newly-built grounds has a significantly higher profile than could have been imagined in 1946. For that there are a number of reasons, including the recommendations of the inquiries after Valley Parade and Hillsborough. Those changes have indeed cost money and the football business has accepted that money is well spent if it is used to create an atmosphere of comfort, security and safety and so retain its customers and attract some more. While it must be right to say that football has learnt some important and indeed vital lessons from its history of tragedy, anyone who thinks that these lessons are not financially influenced or that there could never be another tragedy at a football ground is deluding themself.

66 more deaths at Ibrox in 1971 resulted in another report and more recommendations. Lord Wheatley's report, published in 1972, was the catalyst for the Safety of Sports Grounds Act 1975. That Parliament took as long as three years to pass legislation on the 1972 report's recommendations does not look like an urgent response when compared with what can be achieved in speeding through some legislation. Even then, as we shall see presently, the need for a safety certificate was restricted to a minority of sports grounds. Like Moelwyn Hughes, the author of the 1946 report, Lord Wheatley was far from optimistic about the reaction of the football clubs to his recommendations. He wrote: "I recognise that a decision to introduce a licensing system for grounds along the lines I have recommended may cause anxiety to some football clubs and football administrators. As I see it, their misgivings are associated with a fear that such

stringent conditions might be attached to the granting of a licence that many clubs may not be able to afford the cost and some may have to go out of business."

Lord Wheatley was, however, rather more determined in the face of the likely opposition. He was ready immediately to defend his recommendation and wrote: "My task was to consider the problem of crowd safety at grounds. Clubs which charge the public for admission have a duty to see that their grounds are reasonably safe for spectators. That is a primary consideration. It is accordingly necessary that some standards should be imposed and observed. This has been recognised by the football authorities themselves... I have canvassed all the alternatives that have been proposed or which I personally thought were reasonable to consider, and the one which I have decided was best to meet the situation in the interest of the public is the licensing system by a local authority. There is nothing new in this proposal. It has been mooted for almost fifty years. It can come as no surprise to the football world, and in the light of happenings over the years the demand for an independent appraisal and determination of the safety of grounds becomes almost irresistible. I certainly cannot resist it." Football would apparently have to come into the real world, like any other business whose customers remain in its premises for lengthy periods of time. But football wasn't like any other business, was it? It was a special case, of course.

In the true tragedies in the history of football, people have died. The rest, the other so-called tragedies, are mainly financial. A club has "died", its supporters have lost "a loved one". The list of financial tragedies is considerably longer than the list of true tragedies, but they often overlap. If only more money had been spent on keeping grounds well maintained, on stewarding, on training, on providing better facilities for spectators - if only more money had been spent on any of these things, most of the real football tragedies would never have happened. But we all know that the history of professional football is littered with money mis-spent, whether it be into the pockets of unscrupulous directors, on exorbitant wage bills or on any other scheme intended to get someone very rich very quickly. Over the years only the destination of the money has altered. The spectators have always been the ones who don't matter, so long as they keep turning up at the turnstile. In those true football tragedies, how many directors died?

Burnden Park in 1946 and Ibrox in 1971 are not the only football disasters where fans died. But, as we move on to see how even more fans died at Valley Parade in 1985, it is worth more than just a passing thought to question how little was learnt from those earlier tragedies, how much might have been done to implement the recommendations from those reports and, finally, whether that implementation might have saved 56 lives.

THREE

The stand at Valley Parade was rather unusual. There's no need to ask which stand I'm talking about, because back in 1985 it was the only seated area in the ground. There had been seated accommodation on the Midland Road side of the ground, but various difficulties with the foundations on the steep slope had, despite attempts at redevelopment, brought about its demolition in 1960. Such are the changes to the ground in the last twenty years that no one going there for the first time today would be able to work out just how the stand looked back then. Even those of us who have been going to Valley Parade for over forty years have to stop and think about where the old stand fitted into the space now occupied by its twice-developed successor. The lie of the land remains the same, of course, and the slope outside the ground from Manningham Lane down Valley Parade is just as steep. South Parade, where the turnstile entrances to the stand were located, no longer exists apart from one very short stretch outside the south end of the new stand. The structure that towers over what used to be South Parade is a very different animal from the stand that was destroyed in 1985.

Manningham Rugby Football Club excavated out the hillside in the late nineteenth century to create a reasonably level pitch running north to south. The rugby club seemed to have fallen on hard times and decided that football was the new sport to play. Thus it was that Bradford City played their first game at the ground in 1903 after being elected to the second division of the Football League without previously having played a competitive match. Over a hundred years later they're still playing there, even if from time to time the words "but only just" come very much to mind. Those of us who were used to the old stand would have sworn it had been there all of those eighty years. We wouldn't have been too far out either, because it hadn't changed all that much since Archibald Leitch's original 1908 design.

South Parade was quite flat, running across the sloping land and along the back of the stand. This was the stand's highest point, so that, as soon as you came through the old turnstiles, you were on the corridor that ran just behind the top row of seats. The same level today would bring you out less than one third of the way up the new stand. Once inside you stood initially on a pathway of uncertain surface. It was always fairly dark along there and nobody ever thought of looking down to see what they were walking on. It was solid enough and that was all that mattered. Like South Parade outside, this path ran the full length of the back of the stand on the inside and took the supporters to the top of the aisles down which the seats were reached. From the pathway there was no "up".

The aisles and their downward steps could confuse the occasional and unwary visitor. Without telling you which was which, some of the aisles only went halfway down the rows of seats and thus were a source of frustration for those trying to find a seat in the lower section. Similarly those aisles that did reach to the lower section were no use for those with seats in the upper section. And those who thought any of these aisles would take them down to the front part, the standing area known as The Paddock, were starting from the wrong place altogether. Except on "big match" days, when a brass band might play, the occasional visitor's frustration was what passed as pre-match entertainment for the regulars!

The mystery was solved once you got the hang of thinking of the stand in three sections - the upper rows of wooden seats on wooden floorboards, the lower rows, which by 1985 were plastic seats with metal supports set in concrete, and, lastly, the standing areas. Starting at the bottom and nearest the pitch was The Paddock. This ran the length of the stand and was made up of a few concrete steps, the most recently refurbished flooring in the whole stand. Above and below these steps was a level walkway, again running the length of the stand. The lower walkway was below pitch level by a couple of feet. Thus the pitchside wall, which looked barely three or four feet high when seen from the far side of the pitch, was something like five feet high for anyone standing at the front of The Paddock. Immediately behind the walkway along the top of The Paddock was a wooden wall that formed the front of the lower level of seats. This wall was about five feet high and ran the length of The Paddock, save for the two ends.

At the north end of The Paddock, nearest to the Kop, the concrete steps continued all the way up to the top of the stand, finishing at the pathway just inside the turnstiles. Entrance to The Paddock was via those steps and a separate turnstile from those that gave access to the seating area. There was a large door toward the north end of the top pathway denying access to the seated areas for those who had paid only to stand up. The steps near the Kop were used by standing spectators at busier games and were separated from the seats down their full length by another wooden wall topped off with a metal railing. At the south end of The Paddock, nearest to the Bradford End covered terracing, were more steps from top to bottom and a gents' toilet block. (As we shall see later, there was another gents' toilet off the top corridor. Nowhere in the stand was there a ladies' toilet. Despite the fact that the latter years of the twentieth century were well and truly on the horizon, the football business in the lower leagues still did not see any necessity to provide the most basic facilities for anyone other than the male fan. And it was for this part of the ground, remember, that the most expensive tickets were sold. You should have seen the facilities, even for the men, in the other parts of the ground!) The south end of The Paddock provided what would now be recalled as a restricted view - you couldn't see the goal at the Bradford End from anywhere near the top - and was more of a thoroughfare than a place from which to watch the game. The whole terraced area, then, was an enormous U shape along the ends and the bottom of the stand.

Inside this huge U were the two blocks of seats. Right in the centre of the upper area overlooking the halfway line were the seats reserved for the directors and their guests and, just below them, those given over to the press. That the press were slightly in front of the directors was a minor source of wonder. Maybe the directors just thought their slightly elevated position gave them a better view of the game. Or maybe they just preferred to keep an eye on the reporters rather than the other way round! The rest of the seats in the upper level were little more than flat pieces of wood with a number painted on each seat. They had no backs to them and were divided from each other by a curious grab handle between each seat. The spectators in these seats rested their feet on two wooden planks that ran at a level midway between successive rows of seats. Beneath the planks was fresh air and, as was later revealed, a certain amount of litter resting on the original sloping ground upon which the stand had been constructed.

The seats in the upper level ran from Row Q at the very top down to Row I. Behind Row Q was a wooden wall running along the inside of the walkway at the top of the stand. The wall, about four feet high, was interrupted by the openings at the top of the aisles. In front of Row I was another wooden wall, also about four feet high and this time with just two openings for the only aisles to take spectators from the top walkway down to the seats in the lower level. Those seats were Rows F down to A at the front. Row A was immediately above The Paddock. The drop of about five feet between the lowest row of seats and the standing area was not intended to be negotiated by spectators in either direction. The seats in the lower level had been replaced some years earlier. They were made, technically speaking, of yellow polypropylene and were fixed to a concrete base using metal supports.

The rows of seats were divided into Blocks A to G as one proceeded from the south to the north end of the stand. Or very nearly so. Along the top walkway hung signs indicating which block was which. At some time someone's alphabetical knowledge had been less than perfect and the signs for Blocks E and F were transposed, another little source of frustration or amusement, depending on your familiarity with the ground. In the upper level the numbers on the seats ran from 1 to 151, this time in the correct order. Within Block G, the block nearest to the Kop, the seats were numbered 130 to 151.

The roof was supported by a series of iron pillars joined together by diagonal ties. These pillars and ties were placed with sufficient frequency and strategy to merit the view from the stand once being described by Simon Inglis as like looking at a football match from the cockpit of a Sopwith Camel. One of the tricks when choosing your seat was to avoid those where the pillars blocked your view of the centre of the goal. It was not a particularly difficult trick at most matches in the 1980s, given the considerable choice of available seats.

Another trick when choosing your seat was to find a dry spot. The Valley Parade stand was to all intents and purposes fully covered. Looking up from the seating area into the darkness overhead, it was just possible to make out wooden boarding and rafters. Above that and clearly visible from the outside as you walked down Valley Parade towards the ground was the asphalt-covered tarpaulin designed to make the stand rainproof. And it very probably had been rainproof at some time in the past. For some years the roof was known to leak, a defect especially well known to those who had either sat on a wet seat or been dripped upon during the course of a game. Most summers another patch or two was added to the different shades of asphalt, but the fact that the roof had a valley running along the middle - it was effectively two inverted V-shapes - meant that some water always gathered on it and found the easiest escape route, often down into the seats. The valley in the roof was also a sure trap for any ball kicked high enough and hard enough by the heavier-footed defenders of times gone by, who would be guaranteed some breathing space while a replacement ball could be found.

It had been reported that some bits of the roof had either fallen or been blown off. In any event the state of the roof was recognised by the club to be bad enough to merit replacement. Contractors were due to start on the first working day after the end of the season. Their task was to remove the old roof and to replace it in its entirety. If they did turn up on Monday 13th May, they didn't stay very long. By then the design of the stand - especially its different levels and the void on which it was built - and the materials in which it had been constructed had played their terrible part in the start and rapid spread of the fire.

FOUR

On the evening of Friday 10th May 1985 Val Walsh spoke to her father on the telephone. Val, her husband Chris and their two small daughters lived in Clayton, on the west edge of Bradford. Val's parents, Renee and Norman Hall, lived off Bolton Road, to the north east of the city. Renee and Norman also had a son, David, who was a little older than Val and who lived with his wife in Tingley, over the Bradford boundary and into Wakefield. Not the most far-flung of families, but far enough and busy enough to make daily visits to see mum and dad impractical.

During the course of Val's conversation with her father the subject of football arose. Val had only been to Valley Parade, the home of Bradford City, once and that was when she was a teenager. Her brother was a regular attender of matches and her father was an avid supporter. Norman was, however, 71 years old now and in ill health. In particular he suffered from emphysema. For almost all of the last 25 years he had had to limit his support to cheering on City while waiting for the results on the television. Not that he would have had a great deal to cheer about in that time.

Since the early 1960s, when City were relegated to the fourth division for the first time in their history, they had enjoyed only occasional and limited successes. They had had a couple of cup runs, beating the likes of Everton and Liverpool, and they had three times been promoted to the third division, although on none of those occasions had they finished as champions of the fourth division. In the same period they had twice finished 23rd in the fourth division, forcing them to go through the ignominious process of applying for re-election to the Football League in the days before relegation to the lower leagues was automatic. Worst of all the club had very nearly gone out of business altogether. In 1983, when many lower division clubs were struggling financially, Bradford City (1908) Limited owed £400,000. The 1908 company ceased trading after its very few assets were transferred to a new company, Bradford City (1983) Limited, the directors of which included Stafford Heginbotham, the erstwhile chairman of the 1908 company, and Jack Tordoff, a past director of the old company. Just about the best thing a City supporter could say at that time was that at least we hadn't gone the same way as Park Avenue, our rivals from across the city. They too had gone out of business, but had managed to resurrect themselves only very much further down the non-league structure.

As Val spoke to her dad, the 1984-85 season was about to come to an end and for Bradford City and its long-suffering fans there was finally something to cheer about. City had won promotion and would be playing in Division Two for the first time since 1937. (Given all the changes to the names of the various leagues, it is perhaps worth reminding ourselves that 1985's "Division Two" was immediately below what we now call "The Premiership".) On the previous Saturday David Hall had persuaded his father to come with him to the home game against Reading. If City won, not only promotion, but the championship could be theirs. In their usual unpredictable style, they managed to lose 5-2 to a team whose mid-table position had left them with nothing to play for. Norman Hall's reaction to the defeat was to say to David, "It's 20 years since I've last seen Bradford play, lad, and if that's what you watch every week, it'll be another 20 years before I see the buggers again."

Two days later a 2-0 Bank Holiday win at Bolton Wanderers and some other results going City's way clinched the title. So it was that the last game of the season, at home to Lincoln City, was to be a family day out and a celebration. Even Bradford City couldn't get it wrong this time and Norman rang David at work to say, "I know what I said last Saturday about not going for another 20 years, but the pressure's off, the lads have done it and it would be really nice to go and see the championship presented." David was naturally delighted to arrange a ticket for his father to go with him to celebrate City's first trophy for so many years. He managed to get two tickets in the upper part of Block C, just to the side of the Directors' Box, as good a view as the stand offered.

During Val's conversation with her father on that Friday evening it came out that Norman had a bad chest in addition to his longer-term ill health. Val questioned whether he ought to be going to the game next day in that condition and tried to talk him out of it. Whether it was the long wait for such a celebration, Norman's determination not to give in to his ailment, the arrangements David had already made or any combination of those factors, Val couldn't persuade her dad to stay away from the game. For a very long time afterwards that inability to talk him out of going to Valley Parade haunted her. Less than twenty-four hours later, Norman Hall and fifty-one other souls had perished while watching a celebratory football match. Another four supporters would lose their lives the following week. It took Val a long time to convince herself she was not to blame. It took David even longer. And it's no good any of us pretending we wouldn't have felt guilty about it.

On the morning of the same match another family was making its final arrangements to watch some football. Robert and Sue Hamilton had been married a little over two years and lived in Cheadle Hulme, just outside Stockport. Robert was a solicitor with a firm in Manchester and Sue was a secretary. Although Sue was brought up in south London, the love of her football life was Liverpool. Robert was born and bred in Bradford and had been watching his football at Valley Parade since 1960, except when his studies and his work kept him away from the city. Both of their teams were playing at home that afternoon and so it turned out that sometime late that morning they went their separate ways. Sue took the family car to Anfield and Robert took the coach from Chorlton Street bus station in Manchester to Bradford. Robert already had his ticket for Valley Parade, on Row Q of Block F in the stand. Row Q was the very top row of the stand, just in front of the walkway by which everyone entered and left that part of the ground. Block F was between the halfway line and the Kop end of the ground.

Norman Hall's chronic emphysema and a long-standing back problem meant that he was not able to walk very far. When David had taken his father to the Reading game, he had been able to drive him right into South Parade and drop him off just outside the turnstiles. That was also the arrangement for the Lincoln game, although David knew that he wouldn't be allowed to leave the car so near to the ground. David went to pick up his father from his parents' home at the side of Peel Park and then set off for Valley Parade. On the fairly short journey to the ground David realised two things. First of all he noticed that his car had very little petrol in the tank. That in itself was not a problem, given that there was enough to get them to the ground and that there was a filling station at the top of Valley Parade.

David's second realisation was, at the time, not much more than a mild embarrassment. Whether at his own home or at his parents', David had left his wallet behind and had very little money with him. He found himself having to ask his father for the loan of ten pounds for petrol. Norman was not one for credit cards, but usually had some cash with him. David remembers his father bringing out a small number of notes, possibly up to a hundred pounds, and giving David ten pounds to get the petrol. David filled the car with petrol - £10 bought a lot more petrol in 1985 than it does now - and dropped his father off near the turnstiles at the entrance to the stand. After David had parked the car a little distance away from the ground, he returned to go into the stand with his father and enjoy the pre-match atmosphere.

For a long time afterwards David could not quite dismiss a thought that he readily accepts is irrational and irrelevant. "At the end of the day," he told me, "when my father died I owed him ten pounds, which made me feel bad even though I was aware that all the money in his pocket had been burned in the fire, so he couldn't have taken it home with him come what may." Maybe only a Yorkshireman working in the financial services industry could retain that thought for so long.

David and Norman, like Robert and so many others that day, got into the ground very early to make sure they missed nothing of the pre-match entertainment. There was a band of majorettes marching up and down the pitch. The players came out with placards to thank the fans for their support throughout the season. Most important of all, of course, was the presentation of the championship trophy to the young City captain Peter Jackson, and the manager of the season award to Trevor Cherry. For once, nobody expected to turn up at five to three, have the pick of the seats and be well settled in time for the action. David had even had the foresight to bring a flask of coffee for the two of them, given the length of time they would be in the ground before the game started. In any event, the coffee must have been very welcome given that it was a cold day for the time of year. That same cool weather was later to prove something of a godsend. For so many years the prosperity of the city of Bradford had been built upon the wool trade. On this one day so many of its citizens were to discover the unexpected benefits of wearing a winter coat.

FIVE

After the celebrations, the presentations, the lap of honour and the majorettes, the football match of Bradford City versus Lincoln City eventually got underway. There are those who remember a few things about the game itself and there remains, of course, a video. It happened that Yorkshire Television had sent their cameras to record the championship-winning team. Their senior commentator, John Helm, was also there. He is a lifetime City supporter and must have looked forward to the rare chance to do a commentary on his own team on such a happy occasion. Once the football stopped and the evacuation began, the mere fact that he kept going at all was a tribute to his professionalism. Even then the manner and content of his commentary quite naturally betrayed the extent to which the events he was having to report tore into his emotions.

At first the tape reminds you of how very different a football pitch could be in 1985 when compared with the playing surfaces of today. The pitch at Valley Parade, being cut into and across the hillside, had had a drainage problem for years. That side of the pitch nearer to the stand was always liable to be wettest. Some drainage work had taken place and the grass still bore the scars to prove it. But, as the video clearly shows, the game was played on the sort of surface which the modern players would deem unacceptable. Very soon the tape shows a scene that makes you forget all about the state of the pitch.

Footballers have long memories, particularly for unusual facts and incidents. Two of the players in the City team that day were Peter Jackson and John Hawley. Jacko was the club captain, although he was only 23 years old. He had been at the club from being what was then called an apprentice. He was a local hero, in the usual football sense of that phrase. He played at centre back, where he had what the football writers call a "commanding presence". He was a big lad in every sense. John Hawley was one of the older players in what was generally a very young team. He had been around a bit and, whereas Jacko's days in the top division were still to come, John Hawley was coming toward the end of his illustrious career. During his time as a professional footballer he had played for, amongst others, Sunderland, Leeds United and the mighty Arsenal. Although not quite as tall as Jacko, he was a fit, strong man with broad shoulders. He played up front alongside one of the true Bradford City legends, Bobby Campbell, of whom more later. Jacko and John Hawley, then, spent most of the game at opposite ends of the pitch, but at least both remembered that City were playing towards the Kop end of the ground. This one snippet of information may not seem very much until you put it into its context, namely that the respective positions of these two players were to have a bearing on what happened to them just before half-time - and that there is very little else anyone remembers about the quite ordinary football that afternoon.

For anyone near to the Bradford End of the ground the events that began around 3.40 were for a little time just another example of football's disease in the 1980s. Hooliganism was rife. Even at Valley Parade, where the average crowd that season was 6,627, there had been one serious outbreak of violence earlier in the season at the game against Derby County. Despite that incident, Chief Inspector Mawson of the West Yorkshire Police was later able to tell the Inquiry that "trouble at this ground was minimal". The police and, it has to be said, so very many of the spectators, staff and players, were, however, far more concerned about hooliganism than crowd safety. Before the game started the police briefing was all to do with hooligans and only incidentally concerned with safety. Lessons had been learned from the Derby match in November, where some away supporters had gained entry to the stand and torn up seats in Block G to use as weapons. The great majority of the away supporters were generally penned up in that half of the terracing on the Kop which was nearer to the Midland Road side of the ground, as far away from the stand as possible. In any event, the number of Lincoln supporters present was low and they were not known to the police as any sort of threat to good order.

A few of the home supporters did, however, give the police more cause for concern. There was a small number of potential troublemakers who had moved out of the home supporters' area on the Kop and into The Paddock. The police were well aware of their presence and had more than adequate manpower to deal with any disorder. The most likely form of any disorder was a pitch invasion. Indeed, although no one was expecting any trouble from a game that was essentially a celebration and a family event, there were 144 police officers on duty in and around the ground.

One of those officers was Constable 5163 Page. These days Gill Page is a solicitor in South Yorkshire, defending the same sort of people she was busy arresting in 1985. Her presence at Valley Parade that day was an accident. She wasn't based at the local police station, but, when another officer was tied up with other duties and she happened to be on the right shift, Gill ended up covering the football match. She'd been to the ground before, but somehow on those occasions it had always worked out that the female officers guarded the coaches outside the ground and the male officers were allocated all the duties inside, from where the match might be seen! Not surprisingly, then, Gill remembers rather vividly the one and only occasion when her duties took her inside Valley Parade.

Gill recalls that the primary duties of the police in and around the ground were related to public order. Although she confesses to being no great football fan, she was aware that "they had won something" and that this was more of a family day. Even so, the pre-match briefing was all about maintaining public order and nothing to do with public safety. Gill's recollection that the officers present "were not given any advice in the briefing on how to evacuate the stand" is entirely in accordance with the evidence given to the Inquiry a little over three weeks later by Inspector Simpson. He gave the pre-match briefing that day and, as he said, it was "principally on crowd control". When asked if he had briefed the officers on any procedure for evacuating the stand in case of an emergency, he said, "To give an evacuation briefing I would have needed to know why the stand was being evacuated. And the reason for the stand being evacuated would then have dictated itself as to which way the stand was evacuated." Quite apart from the impossibility of foreseeing the events that followed, there could be no criticism of the approach adopted by the police in an era when trouble at football matches was never out of the news and crowd safety was given precious little thought by anyone, including the football industry itself.

The long-established traditions of the male-dominated police force may have been breached so as to allow WPC Page into the ground, but they were not to be set aside quite as easily as that. Part of the pre-match entertainment for the game was a band of majorettes. They had been on the pitch before the kick-off and they were to return during the half-time break. Who better, then, than one of the few female officers in the ground to ensure the safety of the young girls? And so it was that, just as the majorettes were preparing for their second display, Gill found herself looking after them at the corner of the ground where the stand and the Bradford End meet and where the players enter and leave the pitch.

Instead of escorting the majorettes on and off the pitch at half-time, Gill, like so many others, realised just before half-time that all was not well at the other end of the stand. The first sign she had that all was not as it should have been "was a small amount of smoke and a little bit of disturbance" at the far end of the stand. She set off running along the pitchside track towards "the trouble". Gill Page, like so many others, was steeped in that Eighties culture that said any sort of a disturbance in and around a football ground was automatically trouble of one sort or another and likely to escalate into serious violence, if it was not nipped in the bud immediately. As she set off toward the halfway line, the thoughts at the forefront of Gill Page's mind were certainly not about public safety - at least not to begin with. Plenty of others, for all sorts of different and perfectly understandable reasons, shared her concentration on public order and crowd control.

In The Paddock at the side of Block G other police officers were stationed to keep an eye on the small band of known troublemakers who had deserted their old spot on the terracing of the Kop and who were believed to be the most likely source of any pitch invasion. It was, after all, that much easier to get on to the pitch from The Paddock than from the Kop because at the bottom of the Kop there was a perimeter fencing attached to the pitchside wall. There was no such fencing in front of the stand, something which eventually came to be seen as an almighty blessing. One of those officers in The Paddock was PC Glynn Leesing. Unlike Gill Page, Glynn was well used to football match duties. He was part of West Yorkshire Police's Task Force, a group of officers specially trained to deal with public order problems, ranging from firearms to football. Glynn and his colleagues were to be found at one or another of West Yorkshire's football grounds every Saturday throughout the season.

He was later to tell the Inquiry about how he first came to smell something which he thought was burning plastic. Entirely in tune with the understandable thinking of virtually all those present, PC Leesing instantly thought this smell was suspicious. For a short time he even wondered whether one of the troublemakers had stubbed out a cigarette on the coat of one of his colleagues. The first sign of any real problem so far as Glynn was concerned was when he saw a small number of spectators in the upper section of the wooden seating immediately to his right peering down "at a very small plume of smoke coming through the floorboards". These were the people sitting in Rows I and J of Block G. Because he could see no other police officer nearby, Glynn climbed over the wooden partition dividing The Paddock from Block G to see if he could be of any assistance. He moved away those who were closest to the smoke and knelt down to try to look between the floorboards and to find out what was happening.

Witnesses who gave evidence at the Inquiry all recounted a sight very much in accordance with what PC Leesing discovered. The floorboards on which the seated spectators rested their feet were not tongue-and-groove boards. They had gaps between them, running lengthways along the stand. At different places the gaps varied between the very narrow and anything up to an inch. One witness was to recount how, at a previous match, his son had lost his scarf down one of the wider gaps between the boards. He also realised that below the boards there was another space, in some places sufficiently deep not to allow a fallen item, even one the size of a scarf, to be retrieved. As Glynn Leesing looked down into the gap between the floorboards of Row I, he "could see a very small fire". Others in the vicinity, but a little further away, described in their evidence to the Inquiry "a little bit of flame" or even just a warm feeling to one leg.

Glynn first tried to pull up the floorboards using his truncheon so that he could attack the fire itself. The gap between the boards was too small to fit his truncheon through and he quickly realised he was not going to be able to get at the seat of the fire. While he was still attempting to reach the fire itself, he also noticed something else, namely that his "coat and gloves had started to melt with the heat from below". He was not to be the last police officer that afternoon to discover that certain items of police uniform, depending on the material from which they were made, were not especially fire-resistant. Once Glynn accepted that his attempts to get at and put out the flames were going to be fruitless, he decided that he had to start to evacuate the stand. This proved not to be as simple a task as he might have hoped for. There were at least two major obstacles in the way of the police officer's attempts to clear the stand.

The first problem was that for some time no one, except perhaps the police officers in the immediate vicinity of Rows I and J, appreciated the seriousness of the situation. There was a general reluctance to evacuate anywhere beyond the most immediate area. One witness after another gave evidence at the Inquiry illustrating this. A young man called Anthony Jarvis had been sitting in Row J, seat 144, next to his grandfather. With the game approaching half-time and not being especially thrilling, he had left his seat a few minutes early to join the lengthy queue for a hot drink. Soon afterwards his grandfather was asked by the police to leave his seat. He went to the back of the stand to find his grandson and, in an attempt to persuade him to leave the stand, told him that there was a fire where they had been sitting. His grandson viewed this as nothing more than "pestering" him, especially since he had just got to the front of the queue and was about to be served. So, when he said to his grandfather, "Let me get my coffee first", all he was doing was adopting the view held at that time by so many that there was nothing especially serious or urgent happening.

Just two seats along from where Mr Jarvis had been sitting was Rufus Kolawole. He too had moved to the back of the stand, from where he was able to look over the partition at the back of Row Q and watch the game. He continued to watch "until I looked back and saw this other thick smoke from where I was originally... and everyone was trying to get out through the back stand." Similarly Steven Wilkinson, who had been sitting two seats to the other side of Mr Jarvis, told the Inquiry that after he had been asked by the police to leave the immediate area, his choice was whether to join the snack bar queue or go to the gents'. He chose the latter, but on leaving there he saw "a wall of smoke coming". Even then, he said, "I actually tried to look to see if I could see anything and if the ball was still being kicked about." Now that we can look back and put this delay into the context of the time within which the blaze took hold of the entire stand, we can judge how valuable were even the few seconds which were lost until a significant number of those in the stand appreciated the seriousness of this whiff of smoke.

The second problem faced by the police was the very fact that the game was still going on. This again is symptomatic of the culture of the time. There must have been dozens of football matches in the previous few years where some sort of crowd disturbance had broken out. For the referee to have stopped any of those matches, save perhaps in the face of the most serious outbreaks of violence on the terraces, would have been to give in to the hooligans. This particular referee did, of course, eventually stop this game, once he, like everyone else, came to appreciate the scale of what was happening. But as long as the game was continuing there was a reluctance to leave the stand, supporters having paid good money!

The other, more serious point about the game continuing was that the great majority of the fans in the stand, not being the ones likely to start a pitch invasion, were naturally reluctant to evacuate by going over the pitch wall. In any event, climbing over that wall was not the easiest or most obvious means of getting away from what was still perceived as a small and isolated incident. The reluctance of the seated spectators to leave in that direction was reinforced by two other facts. Firstly, for those sitting in any seat above the row from which the smoke was emanating, the natural reaction was to move away from the fire, that is to stay towards the back of the stand, rather than towards the fire and down to the pitchside wall. Secondly, for as long as it had been there all spectators had come into and left that stand by turnstiles and doors at the back. That was "the only way" in and out of the stand. For all sorts of reasons even those who were inclined to leave wanted to go to the back of the stand. Glynn Leesing and his fellow officers had a huge task persuading or trying to force people to make a different choice.

Glynn's experience at Valley Parade (and most, if not all, football grounds adopted the same procedure) taught him that the gates through which people were used to leaving the stand remained locked until well into the second half of the game. This was a simple expedient aimed at keeping out those who wanted to watch the match without paying. Glynn was also aware that the turnstiles through which the spectators had entered were also locked soon after kick-off. In any event, turnstiles are built so as to allow fans into a ground and not so as to allow them to leave. In short, they turn in one direction only. By now Glynn's paramount concern was that leaving from the back of the stand "would have been virtually impossible". And he was correct in that assumption, so long as we remember the word "virtually".

Robert Hamilton, you may recall, had his seat on Row Q of Block F. He was on the very back row and one block along from the seat of the fire. Robert was far enough away not to be included among those whom Glynn Leesing and his fellow officers were trying most urgently to evacuate. He was also near enough to feel an unusual warmth coming from under his seat. That warmth grew more and more intense until Robert, like so many others, decided it was time to go. By this time Robert was well aware of some sort of disturbance from just in front of him and to his left. He recalls some people laughing and joking, but, having sat in that stand during countless matches over the last 25 years, he was more inclined to think, "I don't know what's so funny about a fire in a wooden stand." Robert decided that the time had come for him to leave, but has a very clear recollection of thinking "the authorities are going to have to deal with this and I'm going to come back and watch football once they've dealt with it". Even with the knowledge he had and the thinking time he allowed himself, Robert's thoughts were not of "escaping", but simply of keeping out of the way of those who would deal with the fire, so that he could then return and continue to watch the game. While he had some understanding of the urgency of the situation, he had still not guessed at the seriousness of it. In particular he had not anticipated the rapid spread of the smoke and flames.

Robert represents an excellent example of the majority of those spectators who would never dream of leaving that stand by going down to the front and climbing over the pitch wall. First of all, he is the model of the law-abiding citizen, not least because he is a solicitor by profession. Being part of a pitch invasion was never going to be in his thinking. Secondly, when you're sitting on the back row and there's a disturbance and possibly a bit of a fire below you and to your left, you naturally get out of its way by moving up and to your right. Being on that back row meant that there wasn't much upward movement Robert could make, save on to that top walkway. It also meant that his choice of escape route was almost made for him.

At times such as this, there are bound to be questions about the decisions people make. Robert Hamilton, I should explain, is a very bright man. Quite apart from being professionally qualified, he has a degree from Oxford University and several other qualifications. But even he had very little time in which to think things through. As he told me, "I decided to get out of there. Quite how I was going to I hadn't worked out. I knew I'd come in from behind, from the turnstile on South Parade. My instinct was to try and get out the same way as I'd come in. I don't remember thinking about whether or not the gates would still be open. I just knew that I didn't want to be there at that time and I'd come back when things had been sorted." Believe me, if a man with Robert's ability can think like that, anyone can be forgiven for an error of judgement at such a stressful and dramatic time. Suffice to say, for the moment, that Robert started to make his way along that back corridor toward the snack bar above the halfway line, just as police officers and others were doing their best to prevent fleeing fans from using that very same "virtually impossible" means of escape.

Back in Block G, Glynn Leesing suddenly realised what a huge job he had on his hands. People about him were finally beginning to appreciate the seriousness of the situation and most were making for the back of the stand. Glynn's conviction that this was the route to disaster compelled him to make his own way to the rear and to attempt to persuade those trying to escape from the blaze to turn around, go down to the front of the stand, drop down two levels and climb up over a five foot high wall on to a track which ran alongside a pitch where a game of professional football was still, for a short time at least, taking place. It is hardly surprising, with all those factors working against him, that Glynn says, "They wouldn't listen to me."

At the back of the stand above Block G was just about the worst place to be by that time. Due to an unfortunate and disastrous combination of factors, the flames had begun to emerge through those floorboards that Glynn had failed to break apart and, although they showed only a few signs of spreading outwards among the seats in that block, the most significant and unexpected movement which the flames made was upwards. Without pretending to understand all of the expert technical evidence later produced at the Inquiry, it seems that any fire needs oxygen to sustain itself. Flames will lengthen in a search for oxygen. These particular flames lengthened at an alarming rate as the oxygen at lower levels was used up. Effectively they leapt upwards and into the roof space. In an area open to the elements, although the flames would have spread upwards in their search for oxygen, they would not have performed this dramatically fast leap. Because the stand was open to the elements at the front and at the side, the fire behaved as it would have done in a Dutch barn. The conditions held the heat in, caused it to rise up to the top until it hit the underside of the wooden roof and then it bounced back toward the tip of the roof, pointing downward. The wind, blowing into the stand from the Kop, exacerbated the problem by fanning the heat upwards more quickly with the result that it bounced back equally quickly. Any picture, still or moving, of those early moments of the blaze shows a mass of smoke and flames curling out from under the front edge of the roof and moving rapidly along the roof towards the Bradford End at a time when down below in Block G there were still only a few seats ablaze within a confined area.

The heat and the pressure of the confined space within the stand combined to keep the worst of the smoke at the highest point, just under the roof and precisely where that top walkway was starting to become extremely crowded. This rather crude and basic explanation of the way the fire spread helps to explain the comments from those in that walkway. Glynn Leesing, for example, says, "By this time I had to crawl on my hands and knees because the smoke was that thick." This is the same "thick smoke" Mr Kolawole described and it very soon became the "wall of smoke" coming from the Kop end of the walkway that Mr Wilkinson saw, moving at speed towards him as he came out of the toilets.

PC Leesing was by now becoming more and more desperate and determined in his efforts to prevent spectators from trying to escape via that top walkway.

The stage had been reached where he and his colleagues, all of them in police uniform, were having no success with mere verbal encouragement. Glynn resorted to physical restraint. He even remembers from his kneeling position taking such a grip on the legs of one woman that he "actually ripped off her tights trying to pull her back". Such was the alarm by this time that, even faced with a police officer taking a grip on her legs, this lady still wouldn't follow Glynn's instructions. To this day that image stays with him, especially as he is convinced that, after she had made her determined effort to get to that very walkway he was trying to prevent her from reaching, she almost certainly died there. If any who read this can identify someone they know as the lady whose tights were ripped by a policeman, better still if the lady can identify herself, so that PC Leesing can be told that she did after all survive, that special piece of detective work would bring to an end at least one nightmare that still continues from the fateful events of that day.

Robert Hamilton, at about the same time, was making his way from his seat in Row Q, covering the yard or two to that same back corridor. He recalls that "even in the short space of time it took me to decide to leave the seat and walk from the back row into the corridor, the smoke was beginning to get thicker." Although Robert also remembers that "people were still treating it fairly casually" at this stage, he also recollects that "the people ahead of me were beginning to slow up; there were more and more people, even as I was reaching the corridor, joining me at the back." As the numbers up there increased, "You couldn't walk at a normal pace." Worse still, "the smoke was getting thicker and blacker and I think the material in the roof was starting to melt, creating this blacker smoke." Robert was quite right to guess that the black smoke was coming from the asphalt in the roof space, which by now had been set alight by the leaping flames. Although Robert was not destined to witness the later stages of that black smoke, it was soon to reach a point where, along that top corridor, the thickness and blackness of the smoke coming down from the burning roof meant that, quite literally, nobody would be able to see a hand in front of their face and breathing would become an almost impossible task.

However badly Robert was affected by the ever-slowing movement of the increasing numbers up there, nothing could have prepared him for his next thought. In the midst of all this, what PC Leesing was frantically trying to persuade others of suddenly dawned on this very bright individual. "I began to realise that the exits were not open and began to have feelings of panic as to where the exit was going to come from," Robert told me. He was trapped with the roof on fire above his head; with seats on fire below him; with flames and smoke moving along the length of the top corridor "faster than a man could run"; with a rapidly rising temperature; with a tightly packed and ever-increasing number of spectators moving more and more slowly; with an ever-decreasing supply of air to breathe; and with no obvious way out. Glynn Leesing's "virtually impossible" means of escape had become reality for Robert and all those around him.

PC Leesing, on his hands and knees in the thick smoke at the back of the stand and failing to persuade, cajole or even force people away from the back corridor, realised that he himself didn't have much more time. The only decision he could sensibly have come to was to make his own way back down those drops, through the blazing seats, to the front of the stand and over the pitch wall. By the time he made it on to the track, his coat had melted and his head and hair had started to burn. Even then PC Leesing, like so many of his colleagues that day, remained first and foremost a professional police officer. Just as he got on to the pitch, he "noticed an elderly gentlemen trying to get an elderly female over the wall, out of the stand and on to the pitch. I ran to the wall and helped him to pull her over and drag her into the goal area." It was to be said at the Inquiry that, of those who died near to the front of the stand, all were "elderly", all were 70 or over. "It is likely," said counsel to the Inquiry, "that those who perished in the stands were those who were unable, because of their age, perhaps, because of their immobility, to get out quickly enough." We can add that they were also those who didn't find a Glynn Leesing to help pull them up and over that wall.

In Glynn's own case there is a very good reason for his inability to rescue any more spectators. Having helped pull one lady on to the pitch, he immediately went back to assist others. He was particularly anxious to relocate the "elderly gentleman", but by this time Glynn had lost sight of him "and virtually all the people that were in there". Those few seconds, perhaps some of them lost while the seriousness of the situation struck home, really were the occasion when football was a matter of life and death. "It was at this time the roof collapsed on top of me, knocking me out, for a very short while," Glynn recalls. However long that "very short while" was, the next thing Glynn can remember is the inside of an ambulance and a trip to the Bradford Royal Infirmary, where he was to be detained for a week with concussion and burns to his head.

SIX

When the Inquiry began on 5th June 1985, counsel to the Inquiry, Andrew Collins Q.C. (now himself a High Court Judge), said in his opening, "That perhaps is the one good thing that can be said to have come out of this disaster - the bravery and devotion to duty shown by police officers and others in assisting people in escaping from this dreadful blaze." We have seen already the actions of one police officer, PC Leesing, and elsewhere I have recorded separately and at some length what one spectator, Dave Hustler, did that afternoon. Neither of these men would want to be singled out as exceptional. Dave, for example, insists to this day that he did only what anybody else would have done. If Glynn Leesing's wife and daughters read this, I suspect they will learn something about Glynn that he's never told them much about. Many others made their own contributions and I can only write about a few of them.

During the Inquiry PC Sullivan gave evidence of helping Inspector Slocombe to pull an elderly lady over the wall. The fire had by this time spread even at the lower level such that, as this lady was being pulled out of the stand, the back of her clothes was on fire. "The fabric of the woman's clothes was melting. It was like a synthetic fabric and it was melting on to my hands." Just to stay for as long as he did in a position where he could help with such a rescue, PC Sullivan had had to adopt a most unusual way of wearing his police uniform. He was, he told the Inquiry, wearing a flat police hat at the time. He had pulled the hat right down over his ears to protect himself from the heat. It was, indeed, a common feature that many of those injured suffered burns to the tops of their ears. He had taken off his coat and put it over his head, neck and any exposed area of skin that might get burned. "The heat was so intense that my legs started to tingle and I retreated and regained my composure, and crouched down slightly so that my coat was covering the top part of my legs," he told the Inquiry.

Near to PC Sullivan was Inspector Wood. When he gave his evidence, he brought home the extent to which the heat, rather than the flames or the smoke, was driving back those officers standing on the pitch side trying desperately to rescue spectators struggling to climb that last wall. "The heat was so intense that it was not possible to remain at the wall for any length of time and the only way that people could be assisted when it got to that stage was by pulling your coat over your head, dashing in and dashing out, hopefully grabbing somebody while doing it." For PC Thompson, "The heat was so unbearable while you were in the stand, once I had got over the wall I took my raincoat off and put it over my head and pulled people over the wall that were still left on the wall." This was no time for gentility. "We actually picked them up and threw them over the wall. If they were on the top of the wall they got pushed over the wall."

PC Lyles, who had started his duties at the back of the stand with PC Thompson, gave evidence that "The fire developed unbelievably fast. From one minute thinking it would be all right, the next minute the heat was so intense that I knew I was burning at the back - but I knew I wasn't on fire. It was just the heat; it was unbelievable. The time came then for me to get out... When I got over the wall and on to the pitch, I turned round and it was unbearable, the heat was tremendous." PC Frankland, another officer who had been with Constables Thompson and Lyles, also put his raincoat over his head, "but the heat was coming through that as well."

The first police officer to give evidence to the Inquiry was Chief Inspector Mawson. He was the senior officer at the side of the pitch. Although he was eventually to find his way along the entire length of the stand to the toilet block next to Block A, where he and others were to complete a particularly brave rescue, his evidence relates in the first instance what he experienced in the early moments of the fire. His words need no embellishment and little explanation. This is what he had to say about the conditions at the front of Block G:

"The heat from that fire was so intense that it melted the neb of my uniform cap. I got the last living soul out of G block and I think that we are talking about a minute and a half at the outside. Within 20 to 30 yards of that stand it was very, very difficult to breathe and any nearer you were gulping breath and then rushing back out. It was the thickest, blackest smoke I have ever seen. I was conscious of people within the stand moving about and spontaneously bursting on fire. The grass had been burned 22 yards out."

Perhaps the one point of explanation or at least of emphasis about what the Chief Inspector described is the reference to "the heat" rather than to any flames. The wind was actually blowing the flames back into the stand. The burnt grass was the result not of any flames which got on to the pitch itself, but rather from the sheer heat from inside the stand, where it was estimated that the temperature may have reached 900C. Similarly, most of those in that area whose clothing was burning or melting at the back and those whose hair seemed to catch fire while they were standing on the grass had not come into direct contact with any flames. As the temperature in the stand rose and the heat had to find some means of escape, they became the victims of a form of spontaneous combustion.

In amongst these police officers, some of whom were better equipped than others by their more heat-resistant clothing, was John Hawley. John, you will remember, had been playing in the area of the pitch overlooked by Block G. Unlike any of the police officers or other members of the public, most of whom had come sensibly dressed for a cool May day, John was wearing his football kit. Shorts, shirt and socks were of man-made material and pretty thin at that. As the game was going on, John saw people clambering over seats in the stand and what looked like the beginnings of panic. He was somewhat bemused by all this because he "could see only smoke and no real cause for alarm". His reaction was to run towards the front of the stand and, by shouts and gestures with his arms, he tried to restore order.

John's account of what happened next gives another indication of the speed at which things changed and of the need to avoid even the shortest delay. "Then the fire seemed to leap to the roof of the stand and spread rapidly. In seconds I had gone from calming people down to picking them up and throwing them on to the pitch." One of those John picked up and threw on to the pitch was Arnold Whitehead. He had been sitting on the same Row Q in Block F as Robert Hamilton and, like Robert, had made what seemed the obvious choice of taking those few short steps into the back corridor and towards the Bradford End. It hadn't taken him very long, however, to decide that this was not the best place to be once the thick black smoke descended from the burning roof.

Arnold was just two days short of his 65th birthday. For his age he was quite fit - he was still in full-time work and used to carrying on his shoulders what the textile trade calls "pieces", rolls of cloth weighing anything up to a hundredweight. But a combination of the drop in levels in the stand and the rate at which the oxygen was being used up by the fire came very near to defeating him. As he dropped down into The Paddock, he found himself on his haunches and barely able to stand up. An unknown man at his side lifted him to his feet and so enabled him to make the few yards down the terracing of The Paddock to the pitch wall. There Arnold, only some 5' 8" or so in height and fast running out of energy and breath, found the five foot wall one hurdle too many. And there he came face to face with John Hawley. John's powerful physique, the fitness of a professional footballer and, most of all, his bravery were enough to give him the strength to put his arms under Arnold's armpits and bodily to lift him over the wall. It wasn't quite a clean lift, since it cracked a couple of Arnold's ribs. Then again, Arnold was hardly likely to complain about a cracked rib when the alternative was almost certain death.

Although the details are something of a blur, John remembers, "in the next few minutes we helped people out of the stand as best we could until there seemed to be no-one left". Unfortunately, as John and the other rescuers quickly found out, that was far from the case. Again John's description of the next moment speaks for itself. "Then a man appeared in the stand with his clothes on fire, he was walking slowly along the stand and we shouted to encourage him to come towards the pitch but he seemed not to hear us. The heat was so intense by then that I could not get to the barrier at all and even a policeman beside me, though fully-clothed, could not get near enough to help and although but a few yards away, we watched him fall to the floor."

Horrifying as this sight must have been for anyone to see, the realisation that some people were not getting out of the stand then struck John Hawley in the most forceful manner imaginable. John's young son, Adam, was in that stand with three of John's friends and now John started running round the pitch that he knew so well shouting his son's name in his frantic search for the boy. After what seemed to John to be an eternity, he found one of the club's die-hard supporters, who knew Adam was his son and who was able to tell him that she had put him in the goalmouth. John Hawley, who had scored 32 goals for Bradford City, must have had many occasions to celebrate in that goalmouth, but none could possibly compare with the moment he picked up his young son and hugged him.

As John Hawley, Glynn Leesing and other police officers began pulling people over the pitch wall at one end of the stand, WPC Gill Page was running from the other end, still expecting to meet some "trouble". She soon changed her mind because "by the time I got probably to halfway down, the flames were meeting me. That's how fast it was." These flames were not from any burning seats, but from the roof, so quickly had the fire leapt up and along there. As she recalled, "I remember the shock that I had was the speed at which it seemed to be engulfing the roof. I first saw the roof flames. I couldn't believe it. As I was going down running, they were overtaking me coming back the other way. That's the one thing I will never forget. My overwhelming memory of all of that was the speed. It was like a fireball." At this time the seats in front of which Gill was running were not on fire. The burning seats were still some two or three blocks on the other side of the halfway line. Gill was not to get beyond halfway, her progress brought to a halt by the sight of terrified spectators running in all directions, both upwards and downwards within the stand, all trying to get out of the way of the smoke, the flames and the burning asphalt and timber which she saw dropping from the roof.

Gill too joined in, by whatever method presented itself, getting people over that wall and on to the pitch. "People couldn't get out because the other side of the wall was not so low. They were passing kids over... we were pulling people from the wall and there were kids and we were literally pulling them on to the pitch. I think what was happening was that stuff was dropping on people. People's backs were, if they had nylon coats and things on, I think people's clothing was igniting." To the surprise of Gill and her fellow officers, "there were a lot of people I recall who looked fine from the front, who were very badly burned from the back and didn't presumably feel it." Again, most of these people had not come into any sort of contact with a flame, although some would have had melting asphalt dropped onto them. The sheer heat within the stand was the cause of the damage to their clothing and the injuries to their backs. Even some of those who hadn't even been in the stand, but had simply been doing their best to rescue people from the pitchside, suffered burns. Gill recalls an officer standing next to her on the track whose "coat was on fire at the back. We put him out. He'd got one of those nylon coats."

There was something still wholly unreal about all this. Some were prepared, at least momentarily, to believe almost anything, no matter how improbable it might seem later. Others could not believe what was happening in front of their eyes, or at least couldn't believe the seriousness of what they were watching. Arnold Whitehead, for example, having been pulled over the pitch wall by John Hawley, made his uncertain way further towards the middle of the pitch. During his escape he had been holding his spectacles in a way that had left them projecting from the side of his hand. As soon as he began to look for friends, he realised his poor sight made such a search pointless and decided to put on his glasses. As soon as he did so, he realised he had lost the sight of one eye. He had time to think this was a small price for being saved from the flames. Fairly soon, however, his head cleared and he recognised that this loss of sight had a certain improbability about it. Removing his glasses, he discovered that his "blindness" was attributable entirely to the fact that one lens of his spectacles had been covered by a blob of asphalt. As he had reached the front of the stand, molten asphalt had dropped on to the lens and solidified without even cracking it. He picked off the solidified asphalt and thus effected one of the quickest cures for blindness known to medical science!

By way of sharp contrast, Gill Page is not alone in remembering a small group of younger supporters chanting "Let it burn". Perhaps they were thinking that the old stand was due for demolition anyway. More likely they shared the disbelief of so many at that time. Nobody wanted to think of even the remote possibility that anyone might not leave that stand alive. Even among those who watched from other parts of the ground, as the entire stand caught fire from end to end and from top to bottom within four minutes of the appearance of the first flames, no one wanted to believe that people could die just because they had come to enjoy a family day out. And then, as if to provide yet another contrast, at almost the same moment as she heard the unsavoury chants, Gill recognised another group of youths - "I remember I'd locked some of them up the week before" - at her side and only too anxious to find out how best they could help in the rescue efforts. There and then they were rescuers, just like everyone else around them.

By then "there were a lot of badly injured people. I just remember people burnt, the skin burnt completely off on their backs. I think people's clothing was igniting." As if to ram home the overwhelming effects of the heat, the police around Gill Page then discovered that they had not, after all, completed the rescue even of those who were over the wall, on to the pitch, the "people who we thought were in a safe position. Some people who were obviously injured, we pulled them and laid them on the grass and we realised before we got much further that where we'd laid them they were no longer safe, because of the intensity of the heat." Despite the by now obvious burns, mainly to their backs, their heads and the backs of their ears, there was no choice for the rescuers but to move them again. "We were pulling people further in towards the middle of the pitch - the people who were badly injured and couldn't move." These people just had to be moved as a matter of extreme urgency, if necessary dragged over the grass by their feet, both to protect them from further burns from the heat and to make some room for others still climbing over the wall and on to the pitch.

In times of extreme gravity, there are still a few lighter memories that survive. For Gill Page, one of these memories concerns her uniform. Gill, like so many other police officers in the ground that day, had already realised how clothing, including police uniforms, made of certain materials would melt or suddenly catch fire. More traditional clothing provided a better screen against the heat. When she thinks about the heat and what it did to some of her colleagues, Gill remembers, "We had these hideous woollen tights that were vile. It was before any sort of sensible uniforms for women. I remember putting these damned things on. They were awful things, but I was so glad that I had. If I'd had nylon stockings, I would have been badly burned, I'm sure. And I had a gabardine coat on, which again was a good thing. One of the officers with me had a nylon coat and his coat flashed. I always remember thinking that these vile tights were actually a godsend." Small mercies, indeed, but enough to allow some police officers to stay that little bit nearer to the heat for those few moments longer, when even a few seconds could be enough to save another life.

SEVEN

A little further down the touchline from Glynn Leesing, John Hawley and Gill Page was Block C. Block C was almost on the halfway line, slightly nearer to the Bradford End than to the Kop. It was the very next block to that occupied by the directors, their guests and the press. By about 2.15 David and Norman Hall had taken their seats in the upper section of Block C, some two-thirds of the way towards the back. They had enjoyed the pre-match entertainment, the presentations and the coffee that David had thought to bring along. David is just like most other people in having practically no recollection of the game itself until just before the anticipated half-time whistle that never came. "We saw a bit of commotion at the far end of the main stand," he recalls. "We saw some signs of smoke and our initial reaction and those of people around us was that somebody had let a firework off or something along those lines."

That notion about a firework "or something along those lines" took some time after the events to be dispelled. Among those sitting in the press box, a very few yards nearer to the seat of the fire than David and his father, was a reporter from the *Daily Star* by the name of Trueman. His newspaper ran a story on the Monday after the fire in which he declared that, "A smoke bomb caused the tragic Bradford football fire, I am convinced of it, I was sitting only yards away from the seat of the inferno that killed at least 52 fans. I saw everything, every horrifying second, I saw a smoke bomb thrown by hooligans from the stand adjoining the main building and I know that the killer who threw it would have escaped." I have taken that quotation from the Interim Report of the Inquiry. Mr Justice Popplewell's next sentence in that report is, "The article continued in similar dramatic vein."

Once more we have to put ourselves into the context of the times. Hooliganism was very much football's disease in the 1980s. There was almost an assumption, even in the immediate aftermath of the tragedy at Valley Parade, that a fire at a football ground could not be a mere accident. Perhaps there had simply been too many acts of mindless violence and vandalism at football grounds. Perhaps the riot on the very same afternoon, initiated by drunken Leeds United supporters and made worse when Birmingham City fans joined in, was just too close and too much of a coincidence. The outside world may not have wanted to hear too much about the previous absence of trouble at Valley Parade. Trouble at football grounds still sold newspapers. The fire almost had to be the work of some hooligan. Over the next few days newspapers with readerships firmly established among the political classes ran stories about arson generally, about arson at football grounds in particular and about the West Yorkshire Police's view, maintained for a few days after the fire, that a smoke bomb thrown from a nearby terrace, presumably that part of The Paddock where PC Leesing and other officers were standing, could not be ruled out. To be fair to the police, a smoke bomb was never "ruled in" either. They were merely keeping open all the realistic possibilities.

Mr Trueman's evidence at the Inquiry three weeks later was a little different. From 40 yards away and with several hundred spectators between him and the seat of the fire, he described seeing a trail of smoke in the air with a thinner fading smoke from the standing area. People on the pitch, he said, were later talking about a smoke bomb. This confirmed his belief in what he had seen, although just who these people on the pitch were and just what they were saying about a smoke bomb was less than clear. But he did eventually make clear that he "did not actually see anything thrown". The remaining evidence at the Inquiry on this point was absolutely against this version of events. No one, be they fans or police officers in the vicinity of Block G, saw a smoke bomb. There had, in fact, been a smoke canister thrown from the Midland Road side of the ground on to the pitch in front of the standing area on that side of the ground before the game had kicked off. But that was 70 yards away and almost an hour before the fire started. The only other object to be thrown was a meat pie! In proper judicial language, Mr Justice Popplewell concluded "I think the fairest thing I can say about Mr Trueman's evidence is that it is not reliable." Any further suggestion that this fire was the result of anything thrown by a hooligan was firmly put to rest there.

While David Hall was mistaken in his first reaction that a firework had been thrown, he was clearly correct when he thought he noticed some signs of smoke. David echoes the familiar story that "no one initially appeared agitated or concerned". Some time passed before it became apparent that there was a fire, that matters were serious and that David, his father and all those sitting around them, would have to move out of their seats. David and Norman were much closer to the back of the stand than to the front and, if they chose to escape on to the pitch, there were two drops for them to negotiate going down to The Paddock before they reached the pitch wall. To this day David cannot recall why or how they decided to go forwards rather than backwards. His best guess is that even though "there were people going in all directions", they began to move forward because "we could see the open spaces in front of us." Those open spaces had been created by spectators who had already left their seats before David and Norman set off.

"My dad couldn't move very well because of his emphysema. He was a quite big man in terms of weight." Although Norman was little more than average height, he weighed the best part of 14 stone and suffered from a chronic back problem. When David says "moving him was a slow process and a difficult process", he is most probably understating the facts. We have to consider what "moving him" actually meant in this instance. The wooden seats where David and his father began their journey high up in the stand were quite steeply banked and gave little opportunity to obtain any sort of hand-hold. Those seats had no backs to them, so there was nothing upright to take hold of until they reached the barrier that divided the wooden seats from the plastic seats. "We were travelling over seats a row at a time," recalls David, as they made their way to the front of the upper level of seating. At that point they encountered the drop down to the lower level, where the plastic seating was. That was a fall of about four feet, so it is again unsurprising to hear David say, "I had great difficulty getting Father over that."

Their journey would be only about one third complete as they negotiated the partition between the two types of seating, but "already by that time it was clear that things were very serious. There was a lot of smoke, albeit my major recollection is not of the smoke but of the heat. I remember the tar dropping down from the roof of the stand. I just remember the heat. I remember the panic that was all around us." Being so far along the stand from the source of the fire, David and Norman were travelling over seats which themselves had not yet caught fire, but they were under a roof that had long since burst into flames. Not only was hot asphalt dropping on the seats they were trying to climb over, but large sections of the timber in the roof were beginning to fall. All this was happening within three minutes or so of the first flames appearing out of the void under Block G.

David himself is quite a tall and strongly built man. In 1985 he was in his mid-thirties. His strength enabled him to lift, carry or drag his distressed father over the plastic seating area and down the last drop into The Paddock. As David knew only too well, "All there was between us and safety was the wall on to the touchline." But that wall was not as David remembered it. He had told me before we started the interview that he had never been through the events from beginning to end and that he might not remember everything. During our conversation I had mentioned that the pitch wall, perhaps four foot high when viewed from the playing area, was considerably higher from the stand side and thus a much more difficult obstacle to clear than David had remembered. The Paddock steps, although there were not that many of them, took the standing spectator to a level significantly below that of the pitch. Later David said to me, "It's only talking to you today that I have a recollection that the wall on to the touchline was quite deep from the side that I was approaching it." That particular jogging of his memory was to prove a small benefit to David, going a little way toward his understanding of just how difficult it really would have been to pull or lift his father over that last hurdle.

By the time David and Norman reached the steps of The Paddock, "there weren't many people about", a sure sign of how long it had taken them to reach that point and that they were two of the last spectators in that part of the ground. There was, however, another elderly gentleman David recalls asking for help. David himself was left with the invidious choice of offering what help he could to this unknown man or remaining with his obviously distressed and similarly aged father. Either choice ran a grave risk for the man not helped and, worst of all, David could have been caught between two stools with none of the three of them surviving. David was in an utterly impossible position. He can surely be allowed the choice he made of doing what he could for his father, even though that choice meant that the elderly gentleman almost certainly perished after David saw him fall to the ground on the steps of The Paddock.

David's initial recollection of what happened next is both graphic and, it turned out, not entirely accurate. But, just as he had not remembered the difficulty of getting over that wall on to the pitch, again David thought he had remembered a sequence of events which for a time at least increased the sense of guilt which soon overwhelmed him. David's recollection was that, leaving his father at the front of The Paddock, he jumped over the wall on to the touchline and ran to the middle of the field for help. My reminding him of the height of the wall at least partially explained something which he was later told, that he hadn't so much jumped over the wall as staggered over. Once in the middle of the field, as David had initially recalled, "I was imploring a policeman to come and help me." The officer's reply, as David remembers it, was, "Too late, son. No one can get back in there, you're going to have to leave it."

Finally comes that part of David's recollection which, sadly, is the most accurate. "By then my father was very tired, he'd inhaled a lot of smoke, the heat was intense. I guess the oxygen had been eaten up by the fire and we were both struggling." David certainly struggled even to make his own way over that wall. He may very well have implored that policeman for help, but not quite in the way he first remembered. Some two weeks after the fire David was approached by someone he knew reasonably well, although not as a close friend. This man came to speak to David because he had heard him telling people about how he jumped over the wall and ran on to the pitch for help. He too had been at the game that afternoon and had seen David's exit over the pitch wall. He even gave David a detailed and accurate description of the clothes David had been wearing that day, which rightly convinced him that this was not a case of mistaken identity. He told David, "You fell over the wall and you laid there for what might only have been seconds, but it seemed an eternity. I thought you were potentially dead yourself. When you say you ran to the middle for help, you staggered like a blind or drunk man. Obviously the lack of oxygen had affected you." He also confirmed what the police had already told David, that "you were one of the last people to get out of the stand".

It bears repeating that time was of the very essence for so many people, so rapidly did the fire spread. A few seconds in those terrifying conditions really did become a matter of life or death. David's initial recollection that there was virtually no time lapse between his "jumping" over the wall and the police officer's telling him that it was "too late" was clearly wrong. Although it "might only have been seconds", the time which had escaped David's early recollection was certainly sufficient for the police officer's judgement to be all too accurate. It was indeed too late. In the midst of what was by now his own considerable pain, David looked back to find his father still on the wrong side of that wall. "I saw him collapse. I knew he was dead."

EIGHT

As those inside Valley Parade were starting to grasp the enormity of the smoke and flames that were so rapidly engulfing the stand, those away from the ground also began to realise that something major was happening. Tony Lofthouse, for example, was an off-duty fire officer whose house was on the hillside to the east of the ground and less than a mile away. From his home he could see the smoke and the flames. Because he had access to a Fire Service vehicle, he was able to listen to the radio transmissions. They convinced him of several things, not least of which was that there was nothing he could do. He put on his television and heard broadcasters saying, at least in the first instance, that there were no casualties. What he could see and what he could smell combined with his Fire Service experience to tell him that there must be at least serious injuries, probably fatalities. The next day he was on duty and, when he reported to the ground, he saw for himself what little remained of the stand and its last occupants.

Chris Walsh, Norman Hall's son-in-law, had been at home in Clayton that Saturday afternoon doing some work on Norman's car. Chris knew that in order to return the car to Norman's address he would have to drive past the ground and he expected there to be heavy traffic when a much larger than average crowd would be leaving the area just before five o'clock. He planned to return the car and get back home in his own car by not much later than four o'clock. As he drove back home past the end of Midland Road, he could see the last vestiges of a fire. People with blackened faces were leaving the area at what Chris knew should have been just after half-time.

As soon as he got home, he switched on the television and "it was all unfolding". He told Val there had been a fire at Valley Parade and together they listened to the report from John Helm, who had gone to the game with a Yorkshire Television crew to report on a football match and a day of celebration. Chris recalls the "most gripping vision" of an elderly man "with his coat on fire and his hair on fire. They were rolling him on the floor to try to put the flames out." Val knew, of course, that her father and her brother had been sitting in the stand and immediately rang her mother, only to find that her mother knew nothing at all about the horrific events happening only a couple of miles away. A friend agreed to look after their two very young daughters to allow Chris and Val to get across the city to Val's mother and to do whatever was necessary thereafter. Although at that stage they didn't know what had happened, Val recalls, "We realised we weren't going to be back in a rush."

David's wife, Teresa, lived in Tingley and didn't know the area around the ground very well, but she knew enough to get to her mother-in-law's home. Once she reached there, Chris decided to take Teresa in his car and search the hospitals for David and Norman. But Chris's clear recollection is that "We didn't know what had happened. At that stage we thought we'd lost them both." Their first port of call, as was the case with so many families that evening, was the Bradford Royal Infirmary. Chris describes the scene at the casualty department as "absolutely heaving, milling with people". There they began what they hoped would be a fruitful search for Teresa's husband and his father.

Just as Val and Chris were making their way across Bradford, Sue Hamilton was watching her beloved Liverpool players completing their lap of honour around the pitch at Anfield at the end of the last game of their season. As she and her brother began to leave the ground, Sue turned on her transistor radio expecting to hear the rest of the football results. Instead of the classified football results from *Sports Report*, so familiar to all football fans, Sue heard a news bulletin about a fire. She quickly realised that the fire was at Valley Parade and that "there may be injuries or fatalities". This was the best information available to the media at a little after 5 o'clock. It was hardly good enough for Sue, who knew her husband was in the stand that was reported as having burnt down in a very few horrific minutes. Sue needed to know much more and was desperate to find out anything that might allay her worst fears.

Mobile telephones were a thing of the distant future in 1985. Certainly neither Sue nor Robert had one. Sue knew there was a police room inside Anfield. She told one officer that her husband was in the Bradford fire and that she needed to get to the police room as a matter of urgency. Then she managed to persuade another police officer in that room that, such was the gravity of the situation, she should be allowed to use one of their telephones. "I just had to know what was going on," she remembered. The only telephone number she could think to ring was the home number in Bradford of Robert's friend from school and university days, Paul, who Robert was to have met at the game. Perhaps before the advent of the electronic phone book in the mobile telephone we had better memories for numbers. Sue at least remembered the one number that she thought might be useful to her.

Miraculously, when Sue made her call from the police room at about ten past five, not only did she get through straightaway, but she was told that Robert was already at his friend's house having a medicinal whiskey. He and his friend's wife, Ann, who had answered Sue's call, were, however, about to leave at any moment and in quite a hurry to go to Wharfedale Hospital, where Paul and his father-in-law were being treated for burns. And so it came about that, although Sue was reassured Robert was alive and well, she didn't actually speak to him for some hours. She made her way back to Manchester to meet up with her husband later in the evening at the bus station.

It was only two days later that Sue's method of persuading the Merseyside Police to allow her the use of one of their telephones became the subject of some discussion. Sue recalls she must have given the police Robert's details and the fact that she didn't know whether he was alive or dead in the fire at Valley Parade. This had clearly been enough to convince them of the truth of what she was saying. But then, on the afternoon of Monday 13th May, Ann was listening to national radio and, expecting by this time another update on the casualty figures, listened to the news bulletin with more than the usual level of interest. Imagine her surprise when she heard that two men were still missing and unaccounted for, including one Robert Hamilton from Greater Manchester. She, of course, knew that Robert was fully accounted for and she rang her husband to ask him to ring Robert so that Robert in turn could account for himself to the Greater Manchester Police. There was at least something approaching a lighter moment in Sue's recollection that, "I was so damned relieved that I forgot to tell them (the Merseyside Police in the control room) that he was alright." Even the Tuesday evening edition of the *Bradford Telegraph and Argus* contained two paragraphs on its front page about the "only one name outstanding" on the police's missing list. The story confirmed that Robert's wife had rung from the Anfield ground. Thankfully, by the time the newspaper was published all those who needed to know had been told that Robert was not missing, but alive, well and very fortunate.

How Robert arrived safe and apparently unharmed at his friend's home, and yet without his friend, is a remarkable story in its own right. You may recall we last heard of Robert making his way along the corridor at the back of the stand along the route believed by PC Glynn Leesing to be a "virtually impossible" means of escape. Glynn's instant assessment was to be proved all too accurate. On 5th June when Mr Collins opened the Inquiry, he said that the majority of those who had been killed had died at the rear of the stand, quite obviously unable to get out. One or two died in the front part of the stand or in the centre of the stand, but the majority of the 56 deaths occurred in that back corridor. Robert himself says, "I was very lucky - I was incredibly lucky," not to be one of those who died at the rear of the stand.

Robert remembers, as he was making his way from Block F along the top corridor, that he went past the snack bar. This must be that snack bar at the back of Block E. There was, in fact, a second snack bar at the back of Block B, some distance further along the top corridor and beyond the halfway line. Robert doesn't believe he reached that far. "Even in the short space of time it took me to decide to leave the seat and walk from the back row into the corridor, which is only a yard or two, the smoke was beginning to get thicker, the people ahead of me were beginning to slow up, there were more and more people even as I was getting into the corridor joining me at the back," he remembers. With the limited space in that corridor and the growing number of people getting out of their seats, it is no surprise that Robert also recalls, "You couldn't walk at a normal pace." Whatever panic there might have been then or soon thereafter, there was certainly no chance of anyone running in that corridor.

Suddenly two thoughts hit Robert almost at the same time. The first, as the smoke became thicker and blacker, was that "the material in the roof was starting to melt". In other words, he knew now that there was not just a fire in the seating area six or seven rows below where he had been sitting, but that there was a second fire in the roof space above him - and not very much above him at that. As if that realisation was not bad enough, a second and more horrifying discovery followed immediately. "I began to realise that the exits were not open and began to have feelings of panic as to where the exit was going to come from." Robert was aware that there were seven or eight people immediately in front of him. Then he heard a voice through the blackness saying, "There's a gate here, we can go through here and we're out". Not unnaturally, he followed those seven or eight people through "a tiny little corridor leading from the rear corridor into South Parade. I think it must have been a kind of private access maybe for the guys running the turnstiles, the gatemen. I don't know how it had got opened, whether it was always open or someone had forced it. I just knew it was my way out. I didn't have to climb over anything or duck under anything."

When he gave his evidence to the Inquiry, Steven Wilkinson also described going through a door into a storeroom where men were counting money. From there he too was straight out into South Parade. The smoke, he said "was just behind us". Once he got outside, he looked back at the stand and "the flames were flying over the top". Mr Wilkinson told the Inquiry that "some people followed us". Perhaps one was Robert. His recollection is that "not many followed me". What had been a "virtually impossible" means of escape was about to become totally impossible as the black smoke made that particular exit invisible and the flames took hold.

Detective Constable Blanchfield was off duty that day and had gone to the match with three boys. Perhaps they were a little ahead of Steven Wilkinson and Robert Hamilton, given that, when they reached the safety of South Parade, they "didn't see any flames at all at that stage". DC Blanchfield's evidence to the Inquiry would, however, suggest he was not very far in front. There may not have been any flames when he and the boys first escaped, but even in South Parade "we were immediately engulfed in thick, choking, black smoke". A very few seconds could indeed make all the difference. There were several other doors along that corridor, some of which were eventually broken down from the outside by police officers and fans who could hear the frantic attempts of those trapped inside the top corridor to force their way through bolted or barred exits. By the time these solid doors were breached the worst had happened just on the inside.

Once Robert reached the safety of South Parade, he spent some time gathering his thoughts. He remembers seeing a parked car just outside the turnstiles, one of very few vehicles which the police had allowed to be left so close to the ground. From the logo and name emblazoned on the side he knew it was Tony Delahunty's car. He was the match reporter for the local station, Pennine Radio, and within a few minutes he himself was forced to stop his broadcast from inside the stand, but not before he had told his listeners about "human torches" on the pitch. Later, when he went to continue broadcasting from his car, he found that it was nothing more than a burnt-out wreck.

Robert's recollection of what happened thereafter perhaps tells more about his mental condition at the time than it does about what really happened. The walk along South Parade to the bottom of Valley Parade is very short, no more than the length of the football pitch. And yet Robert recalls going up Valley Parade towards Manningham Lane, the main road into the city centre, and meeting two of the City players coming back down Valley Parade. Bobby Campbell and John Hendrie were still wearing their playing kit, in Bobby's case with a jacket over his shirt, and were walking towards the ground. Peter Jackson, the City captain, told me that the players had indeed gone from the ground up to the Belle Vue public house, just across Manningham Lane from the top of Valley Parade. There they had met up, made sure everyone was safe and for a short time had watched the unfolding events on television inside the Belle Vue. By the time Bobby and John were walking back down Valley Parade, some significant time must have passed since the players had left the pitch. Robert, however, had a clear and quite accurate recollection that play had still been continuing when he got out of his seat.

Robert now rationalises this entirely improbable timing by saying, "Maybe for that to be the case I must have spent a bit of time in South Parade". Perhaps the inevitable inference to be drawn is that Robert was in a state of some shock. He himself says, assuming he was in shock, that it was caused "not by things I'd seen, but by things I imagined must be happening." This is further borne out by his extremely hazy recollection of his movements for the next half hour or so. He eventually found himself in the city centre, the best part of a mile away from Valley Parade, looking for a public telephone. He must have walked along Manningham Lane and other roads to get to where he was and, although he was very familiar with the city centre streets, cannot identify which route he took. He found a callbox and, just as his wife was to do a few minutes later, remembered the home number of his friend.

For a very brief time Robert faced a considerable difficulty in his own mind. He was about to ring his friend's home, not knowing who, if anybody, would answer. More than that, although they had been sitting together in the stand, Robert had not seen his friend from the moment he himself first set foot into that top corridor. He did not know whether Paul had escaped, whether he was safe or injured. But he had no other number he could think to ring. When the call was answered by Paul's wife, he found that others had been going through exactly the same anxieties as he had. She was able to tell him that she and her husband, by now on his way in a neighbour's car to hospital for treatment to minor burns, had been going through the very same questions about Robert himself. Now that all their questions were answered, she told Robert how to get to her house by public transport, from where she would drive him to the hospital.

Robert's state of shock persisted, certainly up to the time when he reached his friend's home. Soon after he arrived there he wondered why he was being asked if he would like a biscuit. After all, he wasn't known to be diabetic and one biscuit was hardly going to deal with any pangs of hunger. In fact, what was being offered merely displayed Ann's concern about his state of shock. She was, in fact, offering him a whiskey, the very same drink he was taking when Sue rang and was given the news she had been hoping to hear. Very soon thereafter Ann drove Robert to Wharfedale Hospital where he was reunited with his friend, by now with a sticky patch on the top of his head. With a little more sustenance inside him, Robert was then put on to the bus from Bradford to Manchester to be met at Chorlton Street bus station by Sue, still too relieved to think about a missing person report.

Chris Walsh and Teresa Hall had a more arduous and harrowing task on their hands. Their search did, however, get off to the best possible start. Even in that casualty department at the BRI "milling with people", they found David remarkably quickly. He was in a side ward, badly burned. Despite the seriousness of David's burns, they are not the first thing to come into Chris's mind when he describes finding David. His description of seeing his brother-in-law for the first time begins with, "He was sobbing, he was heart-broken." David was for obvious reasons absolutely convinced that his father had died just on the wrong side of the pitch wall. He was not to be convinced otherwise. Despite Chris and Teresa's questioning and positive words, David had no doubts at all. He was overwhelmed by that one shattering thought.

David Hall was not the only person in that hospital to be distraught. Others with their own injuries of varying severity, and still more family members embarking on a search similar to that of Chris and Teresa, were all around. During the afternoon Muriel Hainsworth had been at home with the television switched on. She had no particular interest in football, but like so many others was drawn to the images being shown by Yorkshire Television. One particular image, of an elderly man just managing to clamber over the pitch wall while his clothing was already on fire, will, she says, remain with her forever. Her only link with Bradford City was that she knew her ex-husband took his aged father to games. She had kept in contact after their divorce, but she didn't know whether they were at this particular game. She was relieved when she telephoned her former mother-in-law and was told that her ex-husband's business commitments had prevented either of them going.

Muriel was employed by Bradford Council as a social worker. She was a trained counsellor, although she told me her professional skills provided no sort of shield for her against the natural emotions she felt on watching the painful struggle of those escaping from the flames. A little later in the evening, however, her professional skills did come to the fore. On local radio she heard an appeal for anyone with counselling experience. She made her way to the BRI where she and her fellow volunteers were faced with an unimaginable scene of distress and grief. As well as those who had been injured, some of whom had been treated and some of whom were still waiting for treatment, the families of those missing and injured were beginning to arrive in their desperate searching. Even the hospital staff, clearly doing their very best in the most extreme and difficult of circumstances, were visibly shocked.

Muriel realised that some of those searching for loved ones were being asked if they could identify personal effects, particularly clothing. Whether they could or could not, it was plain they were all "dreadfully distressed", she told me. In her attempts to do what was best, she asked herself the one question; "What would *I* need?" Then she set about trying to provide what comfort and support she could. She and her colleagues stayed there well into the early hours of Sunday. Amid scenes which must have compared with a battlefield hospital, she remembers most of all a feeling of inadequacy. "It was so very big and I felt very small," she told me. At that time it was very much a matter of offering what was immediately available to the one person or family right in front of you and then moving on with almost indecent, but very necessary, haste to the next. There was no opportunity to maintain lasting contact with any one victim. Although some clearly needed more detailed counselling, there and then all Muriel could do was to refer them on to someone who might have more time in the near future.

Both Chris and David share the clearest recollection of someone else also doing his very best to support those same desperate people. He stood out because he was a tall young man wearing football kit, admittedly with a blazer over the shirt. The kit and the blazer showed that he was a Bradford City player. It was, in fact, the City captain, Peter Jackson, known to all as Jacko. Before Chris and Teresa had arrived at the BRI, David had been comforted by Jacko. It sounds so simple to say that the club captain put his arm round David and tried to console him. We have to remember, though, that here was a young man of just 23, trained since school age to be a professional footballer and nothing but a footballer. This was not a professional counsellor or a nurse or anyone of that sort. This was a young man just being himself.

Several members of Jacko's family had been at Valley Parade to see him being presented with the championship trophy. His father and two brothers had been sitting in Block A and his wife Alison had been with their daughter Charlotte, then just 18 months old. Once the referee had stopped the game and brought most of the players together by the corner of the stand and the Bradford End, Jacko had seen the flames coming along the roof of the stand toward where the players were standing and his family were sitting. The players' wives and girlfriends were watching the game from a room inside the clubhouse from where the full extent of what was happening was not visible. The flames and the smoke were out of sight from the window through which they could see most of the pitch. Jacko rushed up the stairs from the pitch to get his wife and daughter out of the clubhouse and into the street, where he came across his father-in-law. Alison's father promised to take Alison and Charlotte home. With his wife and daughter safe, Jacko could concentrate on finding his brothers and father.

One thing Jacko knew was that his father was with Stuart McCall's father. Jacko recalled with obvious pleasure the close-knit, young team which he captained and which had done so well that season. "We were a group of players and parents and family who all stuck together." It was to turn out that Stuart's father, Andy, was one of the more badly burned. For some hours Stuart didn't know whether his father was dead or alive. When he finally located him in the burns unit at Pinderfields Hospital, it was to be the start of regular visits there for Stuart, to see his father and to provide endless cheer for other victims. Andy McCall had been looked after for a time by Peter Jackson's father, which in part helped to explain why it took Jacko over an hour to find him. Even then his father and his younger brother had escaped by a different route to that used by his older brother, who had employed every inch of his 6'4" frame to force a way out from the top corridor.

Like the rest of the players, Jacko had been in the Belle Vue, where he had watched the grim scenes on the television and heard the reports that there appeared to be "one or two" casualties. With this in his mind he went back down Valley Parade to the ground to collect some belongings and, inevitably, to see for himself what the ground looked like. It was only now "it suddenly hit". He asked a fireman "What's the situation?" only to be told, "We couldn't put a figure on it. There are bodybags on the pitch." This young man, one moment hugely relieved to have located each member of his family and to be reassured that they were unharmed, found himself faced with the stark reality of death and destruction in a stand which he had known so well for so many years. As an apprentice one of his jobs had been to sweep it out after games. He even told me that he and the other apprentices, maybe as young as 15, had played hide and seek in the stand. As captain of his club, he was now seeing it totally destroyed and he could not know how many had died and been injured.

Jacko was able to go to the dressing room to recover his club blazer, the one item of clothing people remember him wearing over his playing kit. I had assumed that he had put this on to keep warm and to show that he was the club's representative. When I asked him about it, he told me a different story - and the fact that he said I could repeat the story tells you one more thing about the man himself. It was obviously true that the blazer would have provided more warmth than the thin football shirt he had worn all afternoon. The blazer, however, had something in the pocket that was far more important than a bit of warmth. Jacko was a centre-half and, although a young man, had played professional football for a number of years. Like all centre-halves he had had his fair share of collisions with opposing players and, as a result, no longer had all his own teeth. In those days it was a common practice for players to remove their false teeth before they went out on to the pitch. Jacko had done just that - and kept his teeth in the pocket of his blazer. He simply had to retrieve the blazer and its contents.

In those days Peter Jackson lived in Shelf. His car was still in one piece and he set off, by now alone, to drive home from the ground. On his way home he passed the entrance to the Bradford Royal Infirmary. He didn't actually make it past that entrance for some hours. "There were hundreds and hundreds of people sat outside the wall at the BRI and I thought I have to stop here, there's no way I can go home. So I walked in my kit into the casualty department at Bradford Royal Infirmary." Again I had assumed that, even in such appalling circumstances, he had had the presence of mind to go there as club captain, to represent the club and the team which so many of those people supported. In fact the truth is much simpler.

For those not too well versed in the personalities of football, a word of explanation may be needed at this point. For those who know or think they know Peter Jackson, player and manager, please bear with me a moment. When I saw Peter in the manager's office at The Galpharm Stadium, the home of Huddersfield Town, one of Bradford City's closest and fiercest rivals, he was every bit the young, up-and-coming football manager. He was justifiably proud of his achievements at Huddersfield, not least the promotion they had just achieved. He was also generous with his time and enjoyed telling me about that other young promotion-winning team he had captained all those years earlier. At the time of our talk City and Town were about to play the first of the season's local derby matches and Jacko knew that those City fans who had once worshipped him as a player would be ready with a few choice words (and maybe more than mere words) now that he was the manager of Town. In between those phases of his career he had played in the top division in England, when Newcastle United had paid Bradford City an awful lot of money for his services. Yet Jacko was still the straightforward bloke you can talk football with, who would listen to what you had to say. He could even volunteer that when he came back to play for City the second time around, he hadn't done as well as he should have done. If that was the only memory City supporters retained of Jacko, coupled now with his commitment to Huddersfield Town, then he knew he would be a bit of a villain at Valley Parade. I tried to persuade him that even City fans would see that there was more of the hero than the villain in him.

When I asked him if he had gone that evening to the BRI as "The Club Captain", a somewhat quizzical look came over him. It seemed to me he had never thought of that before, that the question came to him completely out of the blue. "I went to the BRI as Peter Jackson the person," he told me, as if there could be no other possible answer to my question. When he explained a little more, I also knew that there could indeed be no other possible answer. Once inside he "saw some horrific sights". But these were no strangers he was with. "I knew quite a lot of the supporters that died and got injured, because it was such a family club. It didn't attract big crowds. A lot of supporters had been there since I was 15, 16, a kid. I knew a lot of them. I felt I could do some good. Whether I did or not, I don't know. But I felt that I could do some good. If I had gone home and not done it, I would have regretted it the rest of my life. I felt I could do some good, but I don't say I did do by going in there soon after the event. I have no recollection of how long I was there. I know it was late when I got home, but I couldn't leave because I thought it was important that I was there. I saw the people, some quite badly burned, with scarves and shirts on. There were a lot of people there. I couldn't really leave and I can't remember how long I was there."

I don't know if those words of Jacko's convey their full meaning on the printed page. This, after all, is a hard-boiled ex-professional footballer, a centre-half at that, now a football manager, accustomed to talking to the media at a moment's notice, whether his team have won or lost. But in his face I saw the memories of those hours and what it had meant to that young captain. I was relieved to be able to tell him from my own conversations with those who had been at the BRI that night how much his presence had meant to them, how much good he had done. When I suggested that on that evening and in the days to follow he and the other players could have been in the public eye for their visits to hospitals, attendance at funerals, their fund-raising activities and many other things, his response was, "I did go to funerals and officials from the club did. We didn't make a fuss about what players were going or who was going from the club. It was just showing some dignity toward the deceased. I wanted to be famous for being a professional footballer, a football manager, not famous for this reason, no."

As I said before, Jacko was more than keen to talk football, which was just as well that night back in 1985 and for the following days. As soon as he sat down with supporters waiting to be treated or waiting for their friends, they wanted to talk football to him, to tell him how much they had enjoyed the promotion-winning season. Visits to the BRI and Pinderfields Hospital always involved football talk, soon turning to how much the supporters, still recovering from their horrific injuries, were looking forward to August, the new season in a higher division. The memories clearly crystallised in his mind as he was speaking to me, because he returned again to one of his earlier themes, the youth of the team he had captained. "It was a big task that, for all the players, because we were a young squad as well. We had Bobby Campbell, John Hawley and people like that. But besides that a lot of players were younger than me. For younger players to walk into wards and hospitals and be this figure to go in there, it really humbles you, when you saw someone like that and you had your health. For a lot of young players it was very hard. It was very hard indeed."

Eventually that night Jacko did get home to his family, although he has no idea what time it was by then. What he does remember is the press and television reporters outside his house, wanting interviews. He can't even remember whether he gave an interview, so "surreal" did it all seem to him. Nothing could have prepared him for the responsibilities that had already been placed on his young shoulders and for the further responsibilities he and the rest of the team were about to undertake. After all, as he told me with undue modesty, "I was just the captain of Bradford City." And whether he liked it or not, he was about to become someone considerably greater than "just the captain of Bradford City" in the eyes of many people who had the same Bradford City deep in their veins and who drew enormous support from the very players they themselves had been supporting up to 11th May.

Before leaving Peter Jackson's recollections, there are two other little stories that deserve a mention. The first is about when he went back to the ground a couple of days later to collect his belongings. He knew where his wife and baby daughter had been in the clubhouse. His daughter had had one of those plastic drinking cups with a lid and a lip. It had been left inside the brick built clubhouse and Jacko went to retrieve it. All he found was a small circular blob of plastic, about half an inch high. Although the flames had not entered that room, such had been the heat that the cup had just melted on the table. And finally it was never going to be too long before Jacko got back to football-talk. City's first game of the new season was at Carlisle. The players all knew how important it was for the fans, so many of whom had linked their recovery with the desire to watch City play in a higher division. He recalled, "There was no way when we got off that coach we were going to get beaten. We were going to win." They won 2-1 and some of the wounds were healing a little more quickly.

NINE

Chris Walsh and Teresa Hall had been at least partially successful in their search. They had found David Hall being comforted by Peter Jackson in the casualty department of the Bradford Royal Infirmary. David, like so many of those who had been burned, had not been in direct contact with any flames. His head, his hands and part of his back had all been exposed to the searing heat. His back had become exposed when his shirt had come out of his trousers during his long exertions trying to rescue his father. Although David would say that his injuries were not as severe as some who were being treated at the BRI, they were, nonetheless, serious and must have looked quite appalling. They were certainly severe enough to attract attention from more than one photographer. Indeed the first photographer was the object of one of the very few moments of anger which either David or Chris expressed.

Despite medical advice to the contrary, David had discharged himself from the hospital even before Chris and Teresa arrived. He was less concerned with his injuries than with his urgent need to tell his mother that his father was dead and that he "hadn't been able to save him". As he left the hospital, hardly able to see, flashlights from cameras were going off and David threatened to punch one of the photographers. Given, as David puts it himself, that he has never been a fighter and that his hands were heavily bandaged, this was hardly a serious or sensible threat. It was Chris who took charge of the situation, explaining to the photographer that David had just lost his father and persuading him not to print this particular picture in the next day's newspaper.

When he arrived back at his mother's home, David had to lay on his stomach in agony, so badly burned was his back. His sister remembers that "he could barely speak - he was obviously consumed." David himself was totally convinced that his father had died. The other members of his family were not to be so easily persuaded that a man could simply go to a football match and never return. Val in particular "somehow felt that he was still alive". Although by that time David had described how he and his father had reached the front of the stand and how he had seen his father collapse on the wrong side of the pitch wall, he had not actually put into words his absolute conviction that his father had died. Val embarked on a series of ever more frantic telephone calls to the police, to the ambulance service and "to every hospital under the sun". Each call was met with a response which merely confirmed the lack of firm news amidst the chaos that still showed very little sign of clearing up.

Chris decided that he was not ready to give up on his quest to find Norman. David warned him, "You're wasting you time, you won't get anywhere," but David's own conviction that his father was dead and that no amount of searching would find him alive was not enough to stop Chris from setting out on another search of the BRI and beyond. As well as the BRI, he visited St Luke's and Pinderfields hospitals and the city centre police station. Chris told me of one memory that sticks in his mind. "Seeing the same people searching for lost ones. I remember this one lady, she'd lost twins. Wherever we went, including the police station, she was always in front of me." The names of the 56 who died do in fact include two 12-year-old boys. If they were the sons of the lady in front of Chris, it is impossible to imagine how she must have suffered. Not only did the fire claim her two sons, but she also lost her husband that afternoon.

While Chris was driving round West Yorkshire still looking for Norman, Val remained with her mother, hanging on to "this vision that he could be unconscious somewhere and wasn't able to pass on any details to identify him. It was my vain hope that David was wrong, because he was in such a state of trauma and couldn't be 100% sure what had happened." Only when Chris returned and further telephone calls to family members had produced nothing positive did Val finally begin to believe that David was right after all.

By laying him flat on the back seat of the car, Teresa managed to drive David back to their home. Val and Chris got back home to Clayton just before midnight, only to receive a telephone call in the early hours from the police. There was, inevitably, the brief hope that the police were calling to say that they had traced Norman, perhaps finally identified and recovering in hospital. But they were merely checking through their list of missing persons and asking if Norman had been found. Once again any lingering hope had been dashed. While Val says that for her the acceptance that her father had died was "gradual", Chris looks back to getting up later on that Sunday morning and feeling "there was no chance".

Later that morning David returned to the hospital for his wounds to be dressed. Again the hospital sought to persuade him to be admitted as an in-patient and again David refused unless he could be guaranteed that he would be released in time to deal with his father's funeral. The hospital could give him no such guarantee, so once more David discharged himself. Within a few hours Chris and David were at the city centre police station to deal with more questions and to make a possible identification. David remembers a police officer showing him a plan of the stand with crosses marking where each body had been located. David was able to point to two crosses near to each other and just to one side of the trainer's dug out by the halfway line. David knew they were in the right area simply because he remembered the flask which he had taken to the ground with their coffee in it. "I'd actually carried the silly bloody flask all the way as I was supporting my dad and I'd put the flask down on the top of the dug out. Why I didn't throw it away sooner, God only knows." There weren't very many crosses near the front of the stand, but those two David was confident marked the spots where the elderly gentleman, who had asked for help and then fallen to the ground, and his father had both perished.

When David had given that indication, the police officer left David and Chris for a few seconds, before returning with a plastic "evidence bag". He asked David if he would be prepared to help with the identification. For a very brief moment David "thought he meant look at what was left of my father's body, which I couldn't have done". Instead the officer produced from the bag a gold wedding ring which David described as "completely unblemished", the "mangled remains" of a wrist watch and a "charred buckle" from a set of braces. The ring had David's parents' names on the inside. The watch he recognised as being his father's. For David there was now no question about his father's fate. As soon as the events at the police station were related to her, for Val, too, that formal identification was "when reality dawned". And for Chris, "That's when the numbness set in."

During the course of the morning an impromptu service had been arranged at the Cathedral. David and Chris went straight from the police station somewhat hurriedly to meet the other members of the family there. They were so late arriving that they found themselves on the end of one row of seats, very near to Terry Yorath. He was the assistant manager at Bradford City, but better known as an international player who had only very recently retired. Perhaps he was the public figure the cameramen were looking for. Perhaps it was unfortunate that David, such a tall figure, found himself right next to Terry. What was certainly most unfortunate was that another photographer was able to use a zoom lens from somewhere inside the Cathedral to take pictures of David. David remembers that at this time, "My head was bigger and fatter than normal. It was very swollen, so much so I couldn't get my glasses on. One eye was closed up like you would see a boxer's after a difficult fight and the other one was semi-closed." He was also swathed in bandages and still in great pain.

When the photographs appeared in the national press on the Monday morning, David said he scarcely recognised himself. One of his clients certainly did recognise him. Not knowing that David would have been at the game, the client telephoned him to make sure that he had made no mistake. When Val made the shock discovery that a picture of her brother's swollen and bandaged face had appeared in the national press, her reaction was completely out of character, but certainly understandable. She "felt consuming anger about the press with Monday morning's papers", at least for a short time. "I just found that so terribly intrusive that you couldn't go to a church service without zoom lenses approaching people's tragedy." That the pictures were taken from inside the Cathedral and without David's knowledge merely increased her resentment. While Val's anger may have subsided fairly quickly, her calming down may well have been due, as she herself says, to the medication which soon became essential to her survival.

Although the Hall family knew within hours that Norman had died, the bodies could not be released for some time to allow the necessary procedures to be completed. The complete list of the names of the then 52 who had died was not released to the press by the Coroner until five days after the fire. Four more names were still to be added to that sad list. It was almost a fortnight before Norman's funeral could be held and even then it was impossible to hold a normal family service. Such was the interest in the victims' funerals that there was a small police presence and traffic cones were placed in the areas around the churches.

Most of the funeral services took place within a short time of each other. One of Peter Jackson's duties as club captain was to arrange a rota whereby at least two players went to each service. He had to make sure that no one player was left alone, particularly when the younger players were attending. It was on the day of his father's funeral that David Hall found out what had really happened when he had managed to clamber over the pitch wall. At the customary gathering after the service at his mother's home a friend took him to one side specifically to tell him how he had seen David lying on the track and then "staggering" about the pitch. This was one of the first occasions when David had the opportunity to alter his own by now entrenched view of what had happened and to begin the process, not yet complete to this day, of lifting from himself that terrible sense of responsibility for what happened to his father.

Prior to his father's funeral David, like many others who lost family and friends that afternoon and yet survived themselves, was haunted by what he perceived as his own failings. "I had until then felt very guilty about leaving Dad, about not being braver and saving him, even though from a medical standpoint everyone told me because of his condition he would have died probably on the pitch or in hospital because of the smoke he inhaled. But I felt that I'd failed him by leaving him, even though in a sane moment I accept I'd probably have died with him if I hadn't gone when I did." When he described to me his eventual admission to St Luke's Hospital as an in-patient a month after the fire, once again David compared himself with others whom he must have believed had done more than he had. "Seeing the terrible injuries that many people had sustained again made me feel inadequate, that perhaps I should have been braver and that perhaps if I'd have stayed a little longer, my injuries would have been more severe, I have to say, but perhaps I could have done more to help my father."

David used that expression "in a sane moment" more than once while talking to me. The simple fact is that David is a very "sane" person. Over the intervening years he has had plenty of opportunities to think more rationally about what happened and his part in it. I'm sure the right professionals would be able to make a great deal out of David's self-confessed "muleish" refusal to accept any help from the counselling services. Perhaps even more can be read into his admission that "I've never talked to them (his daughters) about the fire itself and I've never talked to them about their feelings about losing their Grandad. Maybe I don't want them to know the answers." Listening to him, it is abundantly plain that he stayed with his father, in one sense, for too long. David would almost certainly not have been injured at all if he had been at that match by himself and had simply left his seat, as others did do, made his own way down to The Paddock that much more quickly and climbed over the pitch wall. Had he tried to go back into the stand at the time he recovered his senses on the track, there was every likelihood that he would have perished with his father, a fate which he can now acknowledge would have benefited no one, least of all his wife and their two daughters, then aged 12 and 10.

Various people have intentionally or otherwise given David cause to believe in himself a little more about how much he achieved that day. The police at the scene assured him that he was one of the last to get out of that block and that it was hopeless to try to re-enter. The family friend at his father's funeral made him realise that he had underestimated both the seriousness of his own condition and the importance of the short time delay after David had clambered over the wall. Even our talk, in which I reminded him of how high that wall really was, inadvertently helped a little to persuade him of the difficulty of hoisting oneself over it, let alone of pulling a 14-stone elderly man over it at a time when the fire was using up all the available oxygen. And yet I for one am still not convinced that David Hall, rational and sane as he is, will ever be satisfied that there wasn't just some small extra thing he could have done which might have saved his father's life that day in May. More relevantly, perhaps, I don't think we should be at all critical of a son who wanted so desperately to save his father and who still looks back on his father's death as his own "failure", even if we might not agree with his assessment.

TEN

When I started the research for this book, I had a fairly short list of the sort of people I wanted to speak to. I had in mind some of those who were caught up in the fire, some family members, somebody from the football club, perhaps a player or two, maybe a police officer or a fireman. I then started pencilling in a few names. As I started talking to all those people who so generously gave me their time and, I have to say, their emotions, I soon realised that there were many overlapping features of the accounts they were giving me. I could not simply devote a few paragraphs to what one person said and then write the next page from someone else's account. I would in large part have been repeating myself. I needed to fit the various pieces of the story together. At the same time it struck me that, as a result, there would be no chapter which was simply one person's account of what happened to him or her. It wasn't until I met Dave Hustler that I changed my mind about that last point.

I was given Dave's name during my interview with David Hall. They had met each other in St Luke's hospital when David Hall was admitted for his skin graft on 10th June 1985. As I was later to discover, Dave Hustler had been in St Luke's ever since the night of the fire. It turned out he wasn't to remain there very much longer, but that's just one part of his story. David Hall told me that, although he had no address or phone number for Dave Hustler, he still saw him from time to time at matches, where they would exchange a few words and a handshake. At this point the Bradford phonebook came in very handy. If you're looking in there for someone called

Firth, you could be a long time ringing the wrong people. There are a lot of us about! Not so with the Hustlers of Bradford. I was lucky to get the right number at the first attempt.

A lady answered the phone and, after a brief explanation on my part, she assured me I was talking to the right Mrs Hustler. It turned out, however, that Dave was away until the following day. I explained that I would like to talk to him about the fire, but only if he felt up to talking to me about it. I had to emphasise, as I did with all those I wanted to interview, that he must not feel obliged in any way and that I would readily understand if he didn't want to be interviewed by a total stranger on such a difficult and painful subject. His wife was confident that he would be willing to discuss the matter with me, although she very quickly reminded herself that there had been an occasion when he had declined to appear on a television programme. I left my phone number, but said I would ring Dave the following week at a time she had said might be suitable. She also told me that he was 65 years old and that he had apparently the appearance of someone else in football, someone she thought might be called Bates. Again I struck lucky, coming up first time with Ken Bates and asking her if Dave had white hair and a beard. She told me he had, although I was subsequently to see for myself that the similarities between the two football men were strictly limited.

When Dave and I finally met in a café bar near where he lives in Saltaire, I'd already told him that my beard was on the way to matching his in colour and that I couldn't say what colour my hair was, so little of it remained. With those descriptions we had no difficulty in recognising each other. Dave wears his 65 years very well. He is quite a slight man, of medium height or perhaps a little less, with an instant smile that you soon realise is perfectly genuine. As we sat and talked I quickly came to understand that this was a remarkable man, worthy not just of a chapter to himself in this book, but of a great deal more in the wider world. So it was that I changed my mind and decided that this chapter should just be Dave's story, for all that it might overlap with what others had already said.

One of the things I thought I knew about Bradford football fans was that, like so many others from those big cities that have more than one club, you were a supporter of one team or the other, but never of both. In recent years, of course, there has been only one Bradford team in the higher leagues. Poor old Park Avenue went into voluntary liquidation in 1974 and had to be re-formed in the lower leagues. But when Dave Hustler was a younger man you could be a supporter of Park Avenue and still go with your mate to watch City the following Saturday. Dave did just that, taking the opportunity to "play hell" at every City game, just as his mate did the same up at Park Avenue. But when the Avenue went out of business, Dave transferred his allegiance to Valley Parade.

By 1985 he had, mercifully, been a regular in the stand for some years. As he reminded me, "If there had been 500 in that stand and they all went out at once, it was a crush." In the earlier days he had taken his children to matches; latterly, and as the children had grown up, he went with his friends. There were eleven of them who, whenever they could, booked the same row of seats at the back of Block E, specially chosen because that particular row was thought to be a little wider than some others. Block E was where the tea bar was and just one block further away from the halfway line than the Directors' Box. Dave would go down to the ticket

The stand at Valley Parade, 1976, viewed from The Kop, showing The Paddock, the lower seating and some of the patches on the roof.

Peter Jackson, Bradford City's captain, holds up the championship trophy, watched by Stafford Heginbotham, the Chairman, to the right and Jack Tordoff, the Deputy Chairman, partially hidden.

Above: The lap of honour before the kick-off and the majorettes, viewed from Block F, Row Q. The seat of the fire was to the bottom left, just off this picture.

Below: The full stand before the kick-off, viewed from the same place.

Above: Police Constable Glynn Leesing clears the immediate area. The only visible flame is still beneath the floorboards near the letter J.

Below: The fire has taken over Block G and is spreading towards the Bradford End, from where this picture was taken. The players are just leaving the pitch.

Above: The fire takes hold and the smoke spreads more rapidly along the roof away from The Kop, from where this picture was taken.

Below: The fire has taken over almost the whole of the stand and those on the pitch begin their searches.

Above: Thick black smoke fills the sky as the searches up and down the pitch continue.

Below: An inferno with flames from bottom to top. The wooden partition between the lower seats and The Paddock remains visible at the bottom of the picture.

David Hall in happier times, a few months before the fire.

Above: Norman Hall in a moment of relaxation.

Below: Val and Chris Walsh, a year before the fire.

Sue and Robert Hamilton,
a few months after the fire.

Police Constable
Gill Page
"relaxing" in full
uniform in 1983.

Dave Hustler, still working in the bread aisle in 2005.

Dave Hustler holding the Queen's Gallantry Medal awarded to him in 1986.

Arnold Whitehead during the evening of May 11th 1985, still in his thick sweater, still holding his spectacles and looking as if he's been somewhere warm.

The author on the same evening, also in sweater and looking, apparently, as if he has just suffered a heart attack. It washed off.

Professor David Sharpe in 2005 at the Bradford Royal Infirmary, taking a moment between patients.

Outside St Luke's Hospital a few days after the fire, City players (from the left) John Hawley, Peter Jackson and Dave Evans after visiting the injured.

Above: The four foot high memorial, sculpted by Joachim Reisner, in Centenary Square outside the City Hall, showing some of the names in the cloaks of the three figures reaching out over the shattered stadium.

Below: The memorial by the main entrance to the west stand at Valley Parade. It gives the names and ages of those who died. The City's coat of arms and the club badge are at the top.

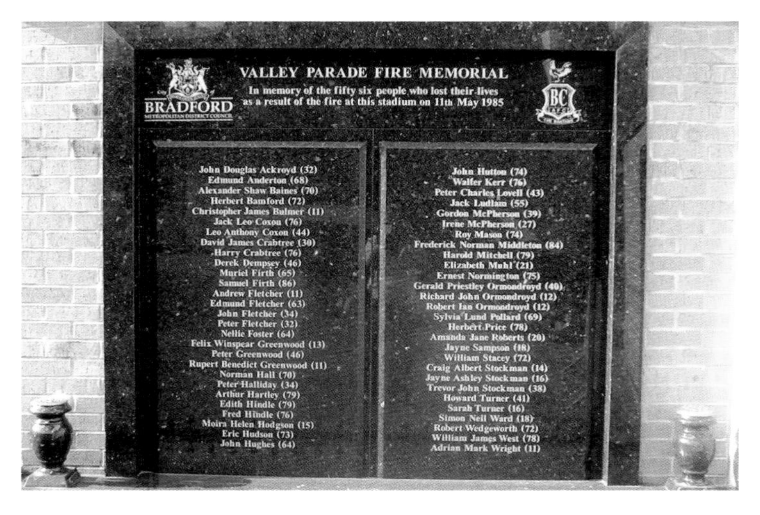

The sculpture by Patricia McAllister higher up the wall of the same stand, to honour the memory of those who died or suffered as a result of the fire.

office to book the seats for the group, just as he did in the days before the Lincoln City match. In those days season ticket holders were not sufficiently numerous to take up all that many of the 2,038 seats, and with crowds that season varying from 3,500 to just over 9,000, Dave managed to book the coveted row Q in Block E for himself and his friends.

The first sign of anything untoward was "just something going off in the far end of the stand", which Dave, in words so similar to those used by so many others, described as "just like a whiff of smoke, as if someone had thrown a firecracker or something". Dave and his friends, along with the great majority of the 4000 or so people in that stand, "just carried on watching the game". There wasn't even any need at that time for the referee to stop the match. One of Dave's friends had no hair and was that much more sensitive than the others to sudden changes in temperature. He it was who called out "Bloody hell, it's getting warm" as the eleven stood up on the back row trying for a better view. They were not to realise at that very moment that the fire had, as Dave now knows, "flashed across the top by then". No one around them had even moved away from their allocated seats.

The next part of Dave's story is remarkable both in its own right and in the wholly unremarkable manner in which he tells it. He and two of his friends, with the roof above them already ablaze, stayed on that back row of Block E, "just making sure people were going forward rather than back up to us". They were acting as unofficial stewards, keeping any number of the crowd away from the area they quite rightly perceived to present the greatest danger - Glynn Leesing's "virtually impossible" means of escape. Even at this stage it must have been obvious to everyone that time was of the very essence. The fire was spreading "faster than a man could run", as the Inquiry was later to be told. But Dave Hustler was not doing any running. "It was not my instinct to run," he told me and then, as if to explain or even excuse himself, he immediately added, "Obviously I didn't realise it was as serious as it was at the time."

Standing at the back of the stand, Dave could see how many people there were in front of him and his friends. He reminded me that "there were a hell of a lot of people in that back", the walkway that stretched the full length of the top of the stand, by now filled with thick smoke and pressing spectators. "My first thought was to get my block clear and to make sure they didn't go to the back," he told me, in that quiet, unassuming manner that I was by now getting used to. "We made sure that they got out. That was the main thing and at least we'd cleared our block," he said, almost as if this man who worked in the Co-op had been emptying a shelf of out-of-date stock. He was almost apologetic that "one or two got injured on the way out", particularly upset that "we had one burnt". That one, his friend Albert, was apparently "oldish" - "but he got out". There were a few other "oldish" supporters in the stand that day, some of whom didn't get out.

So with Block E cleared and the roof above them now well ablaze, the three friends decided, "It's time to go." His two friends were a fraction quicker off the mark than Dave. When he started to make his own way down towards the front, he found that Block E wasn't absolutely clear after all. There, at the bottom of the upper set of seats and sitting on the first seat next to the aisle, was a lady Dave was later to discover was called Kathleen Kelly. Mrs Kelly was 69 years of age. Dave could not have guessed how she came to be in that position. It turned out that she, her friend and her friend's grandson had been sitting together in either Block F or Block G, areas nearer to the source of the fire. They and many others had made that very decision which Dave and his friends had been trying to dissuade people from taking. They had gone on to that walkway at the back of the stand and made their way along it and away from the source of the fire. There had indeed been "a hell of a lot of people in that back", so many, in fact, that their combined pressure had pushed Mrs Kelly off balance when she came to a gap in the partition walling along the walkway. The gap was simply the entrance to one of the aisles leading to the seats below. She had lost her balance, fallen through the gap and rolled down the steps until she had hit the barrier in front of Row I, the lowest row in the upper seating area. There she sat when Dave discovered her regaining some of her composure and, no doubt, trying to get her breath back.

Of course, he knew none of this at the time. Still less did he know that her friend and the young boy had made further progress along that top walkway, fatefully seeking refuge from the smoke by entering the gents' toilet area. This was a brick-built structure with only one entrance and exit. Once you got in there, the only way out was back on to the walkway. I asked Dave if he discovered what happened to this other lady and her grandson. I had always thought there was no way out of the toilets into the street, but Dave reminded me that there had been some small, high-level windows in there to let a bit of light in. Grandma, it transpired, pushed the young lad out of one of those windows and into South Parade. The youngster, Dave was confident, was saved. His grandmother, it seems, was not. The lady Dave found sitting by the aisle on Row I had gone along that walkway together with her friend and the boy. There can be little doubt that, but for the weight of people up there, Mrs Kelly would have continued to stay with them and very probably suffered the same fate as her friend. As Dave said, "How lucky was she to have fallen all down there!"

But all of that came to light much later. At that moment Dave found himself standing over an out-of-breath, confused lady, in the higher section of the seated area and in the midst of a rapidly deteriorating situation. He picked her up and first tried to shield her from the heat. As Dave quite rightly remembered, the partition between the two levels of seating was fairly high and he had to lift her over this and down into the lower level of seats. Dave went one way over the partition and she went another. As they reached the lower level, Mrs Kelly asked Dave, "What about my handbag?" It seems her pension book, her glasses and all the other things ladies kept in their handbags were inside. Dave didn't tell me what his exact reply was to this question, but he did say, "I know what I would probably have said." Perhaps that part is best left to the imagination. Understandably, Dave was not prepared to allow the handbag to be a cause of any further delay. Some time later, down on the pitch, Mrs Kelly felt bound to agree when Dave suggested, "I bet you're glad you left your handbag now."

Without her handbag, then, but still with Dave, Mrs Kelly found herself at the top of the plastic seats. "I just dragged her all over the top of these. I picked her up, threw her, jumped all over all these seats until we got to this point, the big drop down to The Paddock. It was that stage then when the fire was hitting us. So I just threw her over, I just threw her, just into The Paddock at the bottom. I couldn't do anything else. I just dived over head first. Luckily I got up, rolled over, got up, she was there in front of me, I picked her up and threw her over the wall, over the pitch wall. I didn't think I'd got the strength, but in times of necessity I must have had," Dave told me. I said earlier that Dave is not a big man nor especially stocky. That fall from the plastic seats down into The Paddock must have been all of six feet. Once they got down to the bottom of The Paddock, they were faced by a pitch wall about five feet high from the side where they were standing. And Dave was apologising for treating a lady so roughly!

In the middle of all that Dave commented that "the fire was hitting us". The Paddock at its highest point was some six feet below any seating. It consisted of a few concrete steps which led down towards the pitch wall, so that anyone standing by that wall would be perhaps nine or ten feet below the plastic seats and at least as far forward from them. Dave described that position by saying, "Every time you got your head up from there when you were in The Paddock, the flames were going over you. You were all right in there, but when you put your head up from there the flames were going over the top." The heat had been unbearable for some time. The flames had shot along the roof perhaps two or three minutes earlier. The whole place was smoke-logged. Much of the wooden seating area was ablaze. The plastic seats were beginning to melt. The air was getting thinner by the second. And Dave Hustler was still on the stand side of the pitch wall, having thrown a 69-year-old lady on to the pitchside track. Anyone might have expected that he would seize this late opportunity finally to climb over the wall himself. But this remarkable man wasn't quite finished yet.

Another regular from the back row of the stand, but not in the same block where Dave and his friends had booked their seats, was a young man called Matthew Wildman. Despite being only 17 years old at the time, Matthew suffered from rheumatoid arthritis and needed the help of crutches to walk. Certainly his disability meant that he could walk only with difficulty and slowly at the best of times. I would guess that he had chosen the back row of the stand because he could get in and out of there from the South Parade entrances without having to negotiate any steps except for the single step that took him down to his seat from the top corridor. I don't suppose those who calculate evacuation times can make too many allowances for disabled people who, in the dark, the intense heat, the smoke and the flames, are trying to find their way down a considerable number of steps, down drops of four and six-feet and over a five-foot wall.

Another selfless soul had helped this young man down towards the front of the stand. But that man also had his son with him and, not unnaturally, was concerned to find the boy. Although it turned out that the boy was safely over the wall and on the pitch, such was the father's anxiety that he had left Matthew down by the pitch wall. This was where Dave found him as he was gathering his strength so that he himself could climb over the wall and drag the elderly lady away from the mounting heat at the side of the pitch. In the midst of this horrendous chaos Dave heard a voice scream, "God help me." He saw this young man with his chest against the five-foot-high wall, clearly unable to make any further effort to get over and on to the track. "All his coat was on fire at the back," Dave told me. "I just grabbed him and managed to shove him over the wall as well." And now for the first time a very different thought entered Dave's head. After warning so many people not to try to escape by the walkway, after dragging, throwing and generally manhandling one lady and after shoving a disabled young man over the last wall, Dave finally thought, "I've had it." Even as this horror was filling his head, he still had no second thoughts about the young man. In his by now familiarly self-effacing tone, he said to me, "I couldn't leave him. I managed to get to him and get him over."

By this stage Dave had managed to get an elderly lady on to the track on the other side of the pitch wall, closely followed by this disabled young man. He still had time to realise that there was no one in the immediate vicinity on that other side to drag either of them away from the wall. Although the flames and the smoke were contained within the stand, the searing heat was spreading over the track and out towards the pitch. As Dave said, "There was nobody on the pitchside. It was too hot. Nobody could have come in there." The police approached as near as was possible and, by shielding their faces with whatever clothing came to hand, they succeeded in pulling Mrs Kelly away from the pitch wall. Finally Dave himself got over the wall and on to the track.

Once he got on to the pitch, Dave realised that he had burnt his hands. Indeed at that moment he knew of no other injuries he had sustained. He was anxious about his hands because he knew he wouldn't be able to get into work on Monday and the thought uppermost in his mind amidst all this mayhem was "I've got the keys for the shop"! Dave soon found one of his friends, who himself was searching for his own son. For a brief moment Dave thought his friend was going back into the stand to look for the boy and, having escaped from the blaze and the heat only seconds earlier, Dave told his friend that it was "impossible" to go back in there. Fortunately his friend spotted his son on the pitch, leaving Dave with at least one less cause for concern.

Soon thereafter Dave came across one of the St John's Ambulance volunteers. Every football fan sees them at games and maybe most just take them for granted. Nobody who was at Valley Parade that day should ever again have done that. This particular volunteer was assisting Matthew Wildman, now on a stretcher, able to recognise his rescuer and say a few words of thanks. The St John's Ambulance man noticed the condition of Dave's hands. Telling him to hold them out, he poured a small amount of water over them and then asked Dave to stay with him. The ambulance man, it seems, had just been informed that he was to take his patient on the stretcher out of the ground at the corner of the Midland Road stand and Holywell Ash Lane. This was never going to be an easy journey with a stretcher. The Midland Road stand, in truth only a tarmac surface under a low roof, was some way above the road itself. The route down was by a series of steep steps of crumbling concrete and far from ideal for a stretcher bearer.

A difficult trip was made even harder by some members of the crowd. The stretcher had been wheeled to the corner of the ground and then had to be lifted. All those in that corner were "just gawping", blocking the exit by just watching what was going on and, in the process, making the journey out of the ground so much more difficult. So difficult, in fact, that at one point Dave became aware that Matthew was falling off the stretcher as it was being lifted up. Despite the burns to his hands, he took hold of him to help keep him secure on the stretcher and, as he helped lift the stretcher over a barrier, Dave shouted with some justifiable impatience, "Get out of the way, you're blocking the bloody exit." Eventually stretcher and patient made their way safely through the crowd, down the steep stairway and to a waiting ambulance on Midland Road.

By this time there were far more patients than ambulance spaces. Dave and a friend, on the advice of one of the ambulance crew, waited near the corner of Midland Road and Holywell Ash Lane. As they were leaning against the wall, a police car pulled up alongside them and the officer inside it asked Dave if he was alright. With his familiar understatement, Dave told the policeman that he was "a bit burnt". The policeman told Dave to get into the back of the car and quickly realised that Dave might not be able to sit down. The fact that Dave still thought he could sit down was attributable mainly to his own lack of knowledge of the seriousness and extent of his injuries.

He later remembered that, as he finally climbed over that wall on to the pitch, he had taken off all his clothing above the waist. He thought that his clothes were on fire, whereas in fact "the heat was tremendous into my back" and "they were just melting on me". He might have attracted the attention of the police even more quickly if he "hadn't been such a prude". He'd thought briefly of taking off all his clothes, but even amid all the chaos of the pitch side, he couldn't bring himself to do that. As he realised later, however, the cost of preserving his modesty was to prove high. The elastic in the waistband of his trousers and in his underpants had melted into his body. "At the time it didn't bother me, because the euphoria of actually getting out carried me through for four or five hours until it hit me." But the blisters and the burns to his legs and lower body were to hit home as the euphoria faded and normal sensations resumed. And whatever else may have happened that afternoon, the honesty of those on the pitch prevailed. Dave was given back the clothes he had thrown off, albeit "very badly singed, even with a flask still in with not a drop taken out of it, because we weren't going to start the party until half-time."

Back in the police car, Dave and his friend found themselves on the way to hospital by unconventional means. The two friends got into the back of the police car, with a third man getting into the front. By now the streets around the ground were not only full of people trying to escape from the fire and desperately seeking to locate their friends and family, but were further congested by the Saturday afternoon shoppers coming out of the city centre and by the need to make way for vehicles from all three emergency services. The traffic, particularly along Manningham Lane at the top of Valley Parade, was not conducive for emergency journeys.

The police officer set off toward Manningham Lane, as he had to, up a narrow street running parallel with Holywell Ash Lane. That street was "absolutely solid", to quote Dave; so full of people, many of whom must have been in a state of severe distress, that the officer's only means of making any progress was to switch on his siren and drive up the pavement. Manningham Lane was always a busy road, especially at four o'clock on a Saturday afternoon, but the police officer had to make his way across there and turn right. For the second time he decided that the best way forward was to drive on the pavement, by now on the opposite side of Manningham Lane and heading away from the city centre. He drove straight through the traffic lights where Queen's Road crosses Manningham Lane, still going from the pavement at one side of Queen's Road to the pavement at the other side. Eventually he turned left off Manningham Lane into Oak Lane and, for the first time since the journey began, found enough room to drive on the road. From there Dave and his two companions were taken at speed to the Bradford Royal Infirmary. Dave has never been able to identify that officer, but still remembers with admiration and gratitude the "brilliant job" that policeman did in getting the three men to the hospital so quickly amongst such chaotic scenes.

ELEVEN

Thanks to the swift action of the unknown police driver, Dave Hustler arrived at the Bradford Royal Infirmary in the shortest possible time. Even then he described the scene on his arrival as "absolute chaos". But soon the BRI casualty department was to become "very, very crowded". These days all accident and emergency hospitals have plans for dealing with major disasters. I don't imagine such plans were quite as well developed in 1985. A city centre hospital like the BRI would have expected the usual flood of casualties later on a Saturday evening, when the pubs were in full swing. Instead their deluge came early, by some hours, and the task of assessing the seriousness of one burns patient after another must have been nearly impossible. There is more to be said in a later chapter about how this difficult skill was put into practice. Just how well the nursing staff did that evening is reflected in the interim report of the Inquiry, where Mr Justice Popplewell records that "a number of letters praising the work of the hospital staff" were received. Dave Hustler's account of events at the BRI and St Luke's Hospital is one more testimony to the hard work and skill of the staff at those two places.

I'm not sure anyone really knows how many people were taken from Valley Parade to the different hospitals in and around Bradford that afternoon. One estimate, which must be on the conservative side, suggests 200 victims needed hospital treatment that evening for their burns. The number dealt with as out-patients must have been far greater. Certainly by the time Dave reached the BRI, the numbers already present were more than enough to cause delays. The staff could not possibly have treated everyone promptly. Some patients had to be given priority. Dave remembers being asked for his details on a number of occasions and being reassured by nurses, "Just sit down, we'll get to you." There was by now a significant problem for Dave in even that one apparently simple request. Quite simply, Dave could no longer sit down. The euphoria of having come out of the fire alive had kept him going for some time, but by now it was beginning to wear off. As the euphoria wore off, the realisation of how much pain he was in and how serious and widespread were his injuries began to dawn on him. Around this time Dave realised the effects of the elastic parts of his clothing which had melted into his body. For the first time he felt he was "going down and down and down".

As he stood in a doorway, Dave could see a number of cubicles with nurses going in and out, assessing and treating those inside. Eventually, having grown tired of waiting and in increasing pain, Dave spotted an empty cubicle and just stood in it. Nearby were a nurse and a younger colleague, who might well have been under supervision. The younger nurse spotted Dave as he went in to the empty cubicle and alerted the senior nurse, asking her, "What can I do?" The senior nurse said to the trainee, "You've just seen what I've done - you have a go." While this may seem like evidence of understaffing, it is more a reflection of the extreme circumstances of the moment, especially given the enormous number of patients at one time, and of one young lady's willingness to offer as much help as her developing skills might allow. The young trainee came into the cubicle and examined Dave. He was still very much aware of the damage to his hands and, although he was beginning to appreciate that he had other injuries, so severe was the pain in his hands that he and the trainee nurse both concentrated entirely on them. She treated his hands in the manner she must have so recently observed and began to bandage them. As she was finishing this, she asked the senior nurse, "What have I to do to him now?" Again perhaps reflecting the extreme nature of the emergency and the sheer numbers faced by the hospital, the senior nurse's reply, as she was treating yet another burn, was, "Tell him to come back on Monday."

As Dave went towards the door, preparing to "come back on Monday", he met a friend who had just finished his own treatment, again to a burn on one hand, albeit rather less serious than those Dave was aware of. At about the same time Dave "started to go". The adrenalin had stopped flowing and Dave began to think he was finished. He also started to shiver. After all, he had no coat on. His friend took off his own coat and put it round Dave. The two of them made their way towards the exit door, with Dave now reconciled to coming back on Monday.

Before giving Dave the use of his coat, his friend had made a telephone call home, to explain to his wife what had happened. She in turn had made several attempts to contact Dave's wife, but Mrs Hustler had been out. As it happened, while walking back home, Dave's wife had passed a neighbour who told her, "There's been a bit of a fire." He had, it seems, seen the smoke from the football ground in the valley below. Dave's wife obviously knew that he had been at the game and it was perhaps fortunate that the telephone rang again as soon as she got into the house. Dave's friend's wife was able to pass on the information that her husband had given her and Dave's wife went straight back to tell her neighbour where Dave was. Her neighbour, who happened to work at the hospital, immediately volunteered to take her to the casualty department. They met Dave and his friend just as they were reaching the exit.

His neighbour asked Dave where he was going and received the entirely accurate reply, "I've to go home and come back on Monday." The response to this was equally to the point. "You're going nowhere," said his neighbour, promptly calling for an orderly. Not for the first or last time, Dave was asked if he could lie down. By now Dave was finally beginning to realise the extent of his burns and even he was a little more cautious in his reply, saying, "Probably I can on my front." On his front it was, then, that Dave was taken back into the hospital and to a ward where he was put into a bed. And now, for the first time and perhaps some three hours after he had climbed over that pitch wall, Dave received a painkilling injection. This was about 6.45 and Dave's adrenalin had long since failed to keep him going. But Dave is not one to find fault with those doing their very best in extreme circumstances. "Obviously it was chaos," he told me. "You can't blame them. You suddenly get all these people coming in with injuries, it's hard to assess who's got the worst, isn't it?"

The decision was made that the ward to which Dave had been taken should be cleared of all patients who had not been brought from Valley Parade. Dave himself spent that Saturday night drifting in and out of consciousness. He can recall some of the activity, such as nurses bringing in so many medicines for the next day that they covered the centre of the ward. He could describe the scene to me only by saying it was "bloody horrendous". Before the night was out, the additional emotional trauma was brought home to those already in physical pain. Vicars and priests accompanied family members as they looked at every bed, every patient, each one hoping to find their own loved one. It was difficult to tell who suffered more, the survivors in their physical pain or the families who didn't find the people they were so anxiously searching for.

During the night Dave recalls the man in the bed next to him waking up and asking where he was. Upon being told that he was "in The Royal", his confused response was to ask "The Royal Standard?" - a public house not far from the football ground where he had been a few hours before. It can't have taken the poor man very long to realise his mistake.

When Sunday morning came the nursing staff began work on Dave's body. Up to this point, such had been his own concerns for his severely burnt hands and such had been the extreme pressures on the medical staff, no particular attention had been given to the rest of Dave's burns. For the next two or three hours, however, Dave simply laid on his bed, face down, while the nurses treated the burns to his back, the backs of his legs and arms and his head. While he obviously retains a clear memory of having these injuries treated, his recollection is overshadowed by what was going on around him. "All I recollect," he told me, "is that, as they pulled the curtains round, there were cameras coming up to the windows, flashing." At least some members of the Press had brought step-ladders with them, which gave access to the windows of Dave's ward. As Dave was being treated for what were still quite serious burns, camera lenses were being pointed at his bed to provide newspaper readers with the pictures some editors thought they would want to see on Monday morning.

The nurse treating Dave's burns was not impressed by the flashes of the cameras. In fact, as Dave puts it, "she was doing her nut". After she had made the decision to pull the curtains round the bed so as to avoid the other patients having to see the burns, one can only imagine the nurse's reaction to having the same injuries photographed for the world to see in the next morning's newspapers. Dave himself was helpless and just had to lie there while the nurses sorted him out and tried to have the photographers removed. If he thought his encounters with the Press were over, Dave was soon going to have to think again.

The medical teams were by now making decisions on which patients were to be treated in the longer term at the available hospitals. Essentially, those on Dave's ward at the BRI were to be transferred either to St Luke's Hospital in Bradford or to Pinderfields Hospital in Wakefield, where the regional burns unit was situated. The nature of Dave's injuries meant that he was allocated one of the 80 beds which had been set aside at St Luke's and he was moved across the city later on that Sunday.

Installed in his new ward away from the flashing cameras outside the BRI, Dave must have thought that his unsolicited and one-sided dealings with the Press were at an end. The exact opposite soon proved to be the case. Within hours of Dave's arrival at St Luke's, the Press interest started all over again - and this time not just from outside the windows. "All of a sudden the Press rushed through the doors," Dave told me. Each of the reporters "grabbed somebody to talk to" from their captive audience. The one who sat on Dave's bed started asking him about what had happened and Dave, unable to escape and finding little alternative, began to give such an account as he could of what had happened to him on the previous afternoon. The Press were, unsurprisingly, not welcome to the hospital authorities and it didn't take long before security arrived and removed the unwanted visitors with little or no ceremony.

Soon after the Press had been removed by security, Dave was approached by one of the senior hospital managers. The Press were hardly likely to go away and the hospital inevitably had to balance the patients' needs against the wishes of the reporters. Some negotiations had been held and the hospital manager wondered whether Dave would be prepared, for the sake of a more general peace and quiet thereafter, to talk to some members of the Press. It seems that in the short time before the arrival of the security staff, the press had picked out Dave as being a man with a story worth listening to and a man capable of telling his story. By this time Dave had been made comfortable, propped up by numerous pillows, not quite lying and not quite sitting. The work that had been done on his back meant that he no longer had to lie face down. His hands and arms, however, were being held in what was known as a Bradford Sling, of which more in another chapter. But for now, if you picture the upper arm going out horizontally from the shoulder and then the lower arm and hand going up vertically from the elbow, you have an idea of how Dave was perhaps less than entirely comfortable. Then you have to double that image, given that both of his hands were burnt.

As I said at the start of the previous chapter, I'd never met Dave before our interview. Even as he described for me some obviously painful events, I saw in his eyes an occasional glint which I couldn't quite identify. Sometimes I thought it was the beginning of a tear, so much so that once or twice I asked if he felt able to carry on. He always insisted he was fine - although I wasn't entirely convinced - and that it was nothing more than a fond memory bringing a tear of happiness. At other times I was sure it was real joy at recalling some small part of a sequence of tragic events, a recollection that in itself lightened the moment and revealed a little bit more about this unique man. Back on that fateful day, Dave had been so utterly responsible and selfless in his thoughts and actions. As we talked I thought I noticed another, rather mischievous side to his personality. I don't think I was imagining it.

Despite this degree of "comfort", Dave readily agreed to speak to the Press. Whether it be the day after the event or twenty years later, talking about the fire has never been a problem for Dave. He did his interview and, when told that one of the papers which would run the story would be *The Sun*, he was delighted in his little moment of mischief to note that he had been interviewed and photographed topless. He looked forward to seeing himself on page three! Dave was beginning to become something of a personality. He did, however, also tell me that his face was not exactly in the sort of condition that *Sun* readers would expect for their page three pictures. But, being Dave, he quickly told me that, once the scabbing came off his face, "it was all right, so I was lucky that way."

On the Tuesday after the fire the news was being made by Mr Justice Popplewell. On the Monday he had been appointed to chair the Inquiry into the fire at Valley Parade. Simply because they had happened on the same day and at another football match, the Inquiry team was also asked to look into the events at Birmingham City's St Andrew's ground, where a 15-year-old boy had died after a wall had collapsed during serious crowd disorder, ironically involving supporters of Leeds United. Sir Oliver Popplewell arrived in West Yorkshire on that Tuesday morning. Dave Hustler knew nothing about this, since that was the day on which the surgeons went to work on his hands. Grafts were taken from the front of his thighs, one of the few areas of his skin of any significant size not to have been burnt. The rest of the events of the day are lost to Dave's anaesthesia.

From there on Dave underwent daily and sometimes twice-daily treatment. As he tells the tale of the physiotherapist, once more that light comes into his eyes. He was, as he puts it, "a captive audience". Quite simply, unlike many of the other patients in that ward, he couldn't get away from the approaching physiotherapist. Dave insists that she was all of 6' 2" tall and could easily be seen on her approach across the courtyard. By the time she arrived Dave reckons he was the only patient left in the ward. The toilets were particularly well used, it seems. With both hands held high in his Bradford Sling, Dave's first given objective was to try to move his fingers from the top. A man who had just saved human lives in an inferno was not going to be beaten by physiotherapy, no matter how painful it might be. "I'd take the tears and the pain," he said. He even took double the pain. In an attempt to catch up with some of the more elusive patients the physio would make a second, sneaky visit to the ward each afternoon. For the other patients this was their only treatment of the day. Dave was so determined to get back home as soon as possible that he asked for another dose of tears and pain.

The extent of Dave's injuries was such that he couldn't get out of bed for some days. During that period of confinement his ward was the magnet for a vast range of visitors. Some were perhaps better known than others. Some may have come primarily for the publicity or just out of a formal sense of duty. But to Dave they were all to be treated with good humour, even if Dave's humour almost got him into trouble. Dave couldn't move his hands. As he told, "My hands were up here. I couldn't do a thing for myself. I couldn't open my post. I couldn't hold a newspaper. The nurses had to do everything for me. I mean everything." That is until one day when an important-looking gentleman sat at the side of Dave's bed and asked the simple question, "Can I do anything?" Now the most obvious conclusion I drew was that Dave's visitor was not a fellow Yorkshireman. Any Tyke would have spotted the joke. But when Dave replied, "Yes, you see that bottle on the top there, could you put it at the end of there, please?" his visitor's face changed colour just for the couple of seconds it took Dave to admit that he was only joking. His visitor, thankfully, was not unduly put out by Dave's joke. He later asked if the hospital needed any equipment and soon thereafter two special beds and some left-handed surgical equipment arrived. His visitor and the hospital's benefactor was, in fact, a director of another football club. His name was Robert Maxwell.

A chance conversation with the hospital staff then very nearly provoked a security alarm. The patients had been told who the next important visitor was to be and Dave, referring to Mr Maxwell's visit, happened to say, "He wouldn't put the bottle on there, you know, but Maggie will do it for me." The next visitor was indeed to be the Prime Minister. Maybe the hospital wasn't quite sure how to take Dave, but he recalls his bed was surrounded by staff when the PM arrived. But the man who had been apologetic for his rough treatment while saving the life of one lady was never going to be rude to another. Dave had a long chat with Mrs Thatcher and recalls one particular piece of "handbagging" while she was in the ward. The patients had been told she would be on a limited timetable, and it soon became obvious she was talking at length with each one of them. When one of the Prime Minister's aides whispered that she really ought to be moving on, she made it quite plain who would be making that sort of decision!

There could hardly be a greater contrast in the personalities of the two visitors who each earned Dave's greatest respect. The first was the Prime Minister herself, who, as Dave says, "really meant it and really wasn't upset about being with you." The other was a very regular visitor during Dave's one-month stay. He was a gruff Irishman, with a bit of a reputation for liking a drink and even, years before, a conviction for violence. As a youth he had disgraced himself by being involved in the taking of a motor car while representing his country on an overseas football trip. And yet for Dave Hustler and thousands of other Bradford City supporters he was and still is the archetypal football hero. His name is Bobby Campbell.

Bobby had been playing on the afternoon of the fire. Indeed he played in all 46 of City's league games that season and his 23 goals were a very significant contribution towards winning the championship. He has scored more goals for Bradford City in his career than any other player. At any football club that's the stuff heroes are made of. And so it was that the club hero, Bobby Campbell, went almost every day to St Luke's to sit with Dave and the other patients from the fire. Maybe the attraction was medicinal. The burns patients were, it seems, encouraged to keep up their fluid levels and a brewery had sent in enough beer to fill all their lockers. So it was only natural to offer the regular visitor a drink, even if it was only ten o'clock in the morning. Bobby, not known for refusing such an offer, solved the problem by putting his watch on an hour to opening time and just having the one bottle with Dave. The visitor repaid the hospitality one day by bringing in a cake covered in green and white icing, explaining, "My relatives in Ireland have sent you this over." It can be little wonder that Dave describes Bobby as "a smashing guy" and told me, as if I needed any telling by now, that, "You don't forget, you know." Dave Hustler certainly hasn't forgotten.

With twice daily physiotherapy, a wife waiting to look after him at home and a considerable amount of good humour, Dave Hustler secured his hospital discharge just over a month after his admission, although he had to make daily visits to the hospital for the best part of six months in the course of a treatment programme that lasted two years in all. Another immense source of support for Dave was "the hundreds and hundreds of letters from all over the world" he received from well-wishers, especially from school children who must have read about his story in the newspapers. His only regret was that he couldn't read them himself. Such were his injuries that the nurses had to hold them for him and read them to him. "Every day that was good medicine."

There are many incredible things about talking to Dave Hustler, not least the fact that he appears willing to talk to anybody at any time and without any problem, recalling not only the horrific events of 11th May, but also the very painful and distressing weeks that followed. When I wondered how he managed to do that, his explanation was typical of the man. "If I hadn't have got that last lad out or gone for him, if I'd gone over that wall, I'd probably be a nervous wreck after that. It would have weighed on my mind forever, if I hadn't have gone for him. I wouldn't have been able to cope." Quite simply, because he did what he did and because he can cope, he's willing to talk about it. But even as he explained that to me, one more thought slipped out, a memory I would have considered unavoidable. "I know another second in there and I'd have been dead. I aren't talking about ten seconds, another second in there, it was that bad. It does carry over a bit. You think a little bit about..." And then, just for a moment, Dave was quiet.

I couldn't leave him without asking whether it had occurred to him in the intervening years that he would have been unharmed if he'd just got out of his seat and made his way on to the pitch at the earliest opportunity. I can't improve on the answer he gave me. "I never even thought about running. That's why I don't have any problems about it, because my injuries I've got, it's my own fault. It's nobody else's fault. It's my fault because I could have walked away from it. So that's why I've no problem. I don't regret that, not at all. That's the price of my injuries [two people who would not otherwise have been alive]. That's OK with me." So now we know. It's his own fault that he that got those injuries. What do you say to a man like that?

TWELVE

As I said earlier, it had not been my intention to devote the whole of one chapter to one person and I've already devoted two chapters to Dave Hustler's story. This third chapter will be very short, but for me at least it has to be included, because it says one more essential thing about this character.

During my interview with Dave, I asked him if anyone, officially or otherwise, had ever thanked him for his efforts that day. Very quickly he told me that Matthew Wildman had given him a clock. It is inscribed with the words "Time is of the essence" and "Thank you for saving my life". It also turned out that Mrs Kelly's sons were in the armed forces, one in the Royal Navy, the other in the Royal Air Force. They each had their service emblems mounted and presented to Dave with their inscription, "With grateful thanks from the Kelly family". Dave's whole manner as he told me of these gifts showed me how proud he was to have been presented with something so personal.

As I left him, I couldn't help but tell him it had been a privilege to have our talk. I was proud to have met this real hero, who in the best heroic tradition was so self-effacing as to tell me that his injuries were his own fault and that he only did what anybody else would have done. But on my way home I started to think what a pity it was that nothing more official had been done. It was only by complete chance that some weeks later I discovered the whole truth.

One of the people I spoke to about the fire was Arnold Whitehead, pulled to safety over the pitch wall by John Hawley. Arnold later sent me an article from a magazine which had been published somewhere around the time of the fifth anniversary of the fire in

1990. The article showed the obligatory photograph of the flames and the smoke pouring out from the roof of the stand. But alongside that photograph was another, smaller picture of a man I recognised. Overleaf was a slightly larger picture of the same man. The only difference from the man I'd interviewed was that the silver hair of the photographs had turned completely white by the time of the interview. The man in the photograph was indeed Dave Hustler.

And with that discovery I just had to read the whole article. In the larger picture Dave was holding the service emblems presented by the Kelly family. I couldn't at first make out what he was holding in the smaller picture, but the caption and the article itself told me. Dave, another civilian and four police officers were awarded the Queen's Gallantry Medal for their bravery that day. The article even described how Her Majesty made a point, when she presented him with his medal, of shaking Dave's left hand, his right hand still being heavily bandaged more than a year after the fire.

For the benefit of those as ignorant as I was, the Queen's Gallantry Medal is a rare award indeed. It has been presented only since 1974 and is awarded for exemplary acts of bravery. In order of precedence it comes (unless you're a police officer or a firefighter) immediately below the George Cross and the George Medal and is the civilian equivalent of the Distinguished Service Cross, the Military Cross and the Distinguished Flying Cross. Those reference points serve merely to illustrate how high the honour is that Dave and the others received.

Now that his secret is out, I know that Dave would want me to make a point of saying that he wasn't the only one to be awarded the Queen's Gallantry Medal. There were five other people similarly honoured for what they did on May 11th. Four were police officers -

Constables Britton and Ingham and Chief Inspector Mawson and Inspector Slocombe. The other civilian to be honoured was Richard Gough, an installation engineer from Shipley, just a short distance from where Dave himself lives. Constable Ingham pulled a lady over the pitch wall when her clothes and hair were already on fire. He then threw himself on top of her in an attempt to put out the flames. Constable Britton had pulled a man over the wall and was attempting to put out the flames which were beginning to engulf the man when his own hair set alight and he was forced to leave the immediate area. Constable Ingham then took hold of the same man to pull him further away from the heat. Despite his injuries, Constable Britton returned to assist with the rescue work.

Chief Inspector Mawson also rescued a man who was already totally ablaze. Inspector Slocombe's initial involvement was such that his own uniform caught fire and he had to remove his tunic. Using the coat of another officer as a shield, he and a spectator pulled someone else from the fire. Lastly, the two senior officers were part of a small group of policemen who rescued three spectators from a toilet adjacent to Block A at a time when most of the stand was on fire and large quantities of debris were falling down on them from the burning roof. Mr Gough, having escaped from the stand, climbed back over the wall when he saw a lady with her hair on fire struggling to climb on to the pitch. He put out the flames and pulled her to the pitch wall. By this time the heat from her clothing was burning his hands, but he continued until he had pulled her over the wall and, with help from other spectators, carried her further on to the pitch and to comparative safety.

These brief accounts of what the five other heroes did are taken from the notice of their awards in *The London Gazette*. At the end of that notice there is the following, which applies to all six: "They displayed outstanding courage and bravery. Despite severe fire and extremely dangerous conditions they acted in a way which endangered their personal safety in order to save lives." In other words, they were true heroes because they knew the risks they were taking. Or, to use Dave Hustler's own explanation, "It's my fault because I could have walked away from it." I still can't believe he said that!

But that's not my primary reason for finishing Dave's story in this way. My real reason is to give that fuller picture of Dave Hustler. Although, if you ask him, he'll talk about what he did, he always undervalues his actions - "nothing that others wouldn't have done". Although he was proud to tell me of the private presentations from those whose lives he saved, he never mentioned his public recognition from The Queen herself. Only when I asked Dave if I could see him a second time, mainly to take some photographs of him, did he spill the beans. I met Dave at work, where he looks after the newspapers and the bread in one of the Co-op stores on the outskirts of Bradford. He'd brought the medal with him and I was able to have a look at it for myself and to take some pictures of it. While we were doing this, right in the middle of the bread aisle, a number of customers came by, some stopping to buy bread, others just to see what was going on. I asked Dave if many of his regulars knew about his bravery award. He just smiled and gently shook his head.

And so I end my account of Dave Hustler with an apology. Dave, I'm sorry if I've let the cat out of the bag and told too many people just how much of a hero you are, but I just couldn't help it. I reckon anyone who can do what you've done can manage to forgive my broadcasting it.

THIRTEEN

Another man with cause to remember that the afternoon of May 11th was on the chilly side was David Sharpe. He lived then on the outskirts of Leeds and had hoped to spend the afternoon in his garden with his wife and children. The cool weather brought his outdoor activities to an early end and, as a result, he was in his home when the telephone rang around tea-time. The call was from the Yorkshire Clinic, a private hospital at Cottingley, some four miles or so north of Valley Parade. David Sharpe was and still is a consultant plastic surgeon. He had arrived in West Yorkshire as a senior registrar in plastic surgery in 1980 in a career that had started at the John Radcliffe Hospital in Oxford and had taken in appointments at Bath, Chepstow and Glasgow. In January 1985 he had become a consultant based in Bradford.

The telephone call late that afternoon was to tell him that the Yorkshire Clinic had a patient with burns to his hands and to ask Mr Sharpe to come and examine him. He didn't ask any further questions, but set off to drive from his home to the clinic. On his journey he passed through Shipley, perhaps within a couple of miles of Valley Parade, and remembered seeing some smoke. His only reaction at that moment was to think to himself, "I don't know what that's about." But when he arrived at the Yorkshire Clinic, he was soon made aware that there had "been a big fire at the Bradford stadium". Although he had his burns patient to attend to, he was also aware of the fact that he was the only Bradford plastic surgeon on call that weekend. His colleague, with whom he would have shared call-out duties, had gone to Italy for two weeks. David decided he'd better make some telephone calls.

Once again we need just to remind ourselves that this was in an era very much before mobile phones and other means of instant communication, except for the telephone that depended on the landline and the switchboard operator. Even the one consultant plastic surgeon on call could not get through to the switchboard at the Bradford Royal Infirmary, such was the volume of calls going in and out of the hospital that Saturday evening. Perhaps for the very same reason no one contacted him at the private hospital. While his immediate priority was to assess the best treatment for his patient at the Yorkshire Clinic, David decided that, with no apparent hope of getting through by telephone, once he had treated his patient the only way of finding out the extent of what was happening and whether he was needed was to make the short journey to the BRI for himself.

When David arrived at the BRI, he found that another doctor, Anthony Roberts, with a particular interest in burns, was already beginning the process of what is called 'triage' (I admit that the only times I had heard this word used was in episodes of *M*A*S*H*. That particular series was set in a battlefield. Maybe the BRI looked something similar that night.) Triage is essentially the task of assessing the nature and seriousness of the injuries to each victim and trying to establish which victims need priority treatment. It was fortunate that the staff at the BRI were accustomed to dealing with burns cases. Although the plastic surgery unit was based at St Luke's Hospital, the BRI held a burns clinic. The nurses, sisters and anaesthetists David found on his arrival at the casualty department had the experience to deal with this work that staff at other local hospitals may well not have had.

Once the triage system was in place, decisions could be made as to which patients should be admitted, which ones could be treated as out-patients and, most difficult of all, which patients should be transferred to the regional burns unit at Pinderfields Hospital in Wakefield. The Pinderfields beds were reserved for those whose injuries were life-threatening or who had major burns. Ten patients were sent there on that Saturday evening. Sadly, but not unexpectedly from the medical point of view, three of those ten did not survive. Another eighty patients were admitted to the BRI, mainly with burns to the backs of their hands and to their scalps.

David was not familiar with the Valley Parade stand and knew little about the cause of the fire. He decided to go to the ground that night to see for himself. He was concerned, for example, that there might have been some foam in the seats, which would affect the way the burns would be treated. Perhaps the easiest part of his visit was his discussion with the senior fire officer at the ground, who reassured him about the materials that had caught fire. By far the most difficult part of his enquiry was the devastation he came across that evening. With some understatement he describes that scene as "not very pleasant". He also recalls his visit as "quite a moving experience", a phrase with huge meaning for a man of his vast experience of the aftermath of fires and explosions.

His visit to the burnt-out and still smouldering wreckage of the stand provided David with the information he needed about how the burns had been caused. That slightly chilly weather had caused the spectators to wrap up, often in woollen clothing. Only their hands, their faces and, for those with no headgear, their scalps had been exposed to the radiant heat. David explained that concept to me by comparing it with the reflector in an electric fire. "If you look at the stadium it was very much like a parabolic reflector. The heat from the flames underneath the canopy was concentrating down on the victims underneath. So what you were getting was the people who survived were having these radiant heat burns to the backs of their hands where they were protecting their faces and their scalps and to the scalp for those who didn't have caps or were follicularly challenged. One or two others had facial burns, but surprisingly few."

By the time David returned to the BRI, the triage system had done its job. Order had been restored and the decisions had been made about who was to be admitted and to which hospitals. To accommodate the eighty patients to be admitted in Bradford, four wards were cleared at St Luke's Hospital. Skilled as they were, the surgeons, anaesthetists and nursing staff could not possibly have operated on so many burns patients within the time they eventually took. They had support from all over the country. David Sharpe received telephone calls from plastic surgeon colleagues who had heard about the fire and the casualties and who wanted to offer their help. By the Sunday morning about 10 per cent of the plastic surgeons in the UK were either in Bradford or on their way. By Monday morning there were enough surgeons, anaesthetists and nurses to staff four theatres and to operate on thirty patients a day. As David puts it, "We had a team."

How the surgery was done is an interesting little story in its own right, not least because, while it was not the most usual method, it worked very well. David explained to me that the conservative way of dealing with burns would be to let the skin die and slough off. This would take about three weeks, after which a graft could be done. The "aggressive" treatment was to wait up to 48 hours for the fluid to reduce and then cut the skin off, putting the graft on in the same operation. Waiting three weeks or so, especially when many of these patients were elderly, would almost certainly have resulted in significant stiffness to their hands. Operating immediately allowed the medical team to have the patients "mobilising" within a week, with a much better result for the long-term. While most surgeons would have chosen the more conservative approach, the available manpower gave David Sharpe and his team the option of the aggressive treatment. They decided to take that option.

Each operating theatre had a team that included three or four plastic surgeons. Some would take the skin for the graft, others strip off the dead skin and others put on the grafts. In order to make the whole plan work the surgeons had to allocate approximately one hour to each burn site. Thus those with burns to both hands could expect to be in theatre for two hours. With that plan the medical teams could work from eight o'clock in the morning until six or seven in the evening for three consecutive days and in that short time treat all of the eighty patients in St Luke's. There was, as David told me "great camaraderie" and "everything seemed to work out". Indeed, everything did work out. Within three weeks 90 per cent of the patients had 100 per cent graft take. Very few had to be re-grafted or developed an infection.

I want to jump ahead for a moment to put in a note at this stage that David Sharpe was later awarded the O.B.E. in recognition of the work he did in the aftermath of the fire. I mention that now because during our talk you would never have guessed at the skill and effort put into this by the whole team and especially the consultant in charge.

David sought to minimise the whole thing. He told me how much worse the problems could have been if there had been an explosion - shattered limbs, for example - or if the fire had been in an enclosed space - respiratory problems, perhaps. He told me how few facial injuries there were. He described the less successful scalp grafts and those patients where the surgeons initially decided that the burns were not sufficiently deep to justify operating on them, but where there was a later change of diagnosis. He told me how the medical team was "very lucky". What he didn't talk about was their expertise and how hard they all worked and he barely touched upon the enormous success of the whole procedure.

Over the next week or two a few more patients arrived at hospital for the first time. They were generally those who at first hadn't thought their burns were all that serious. After those first few days of surgery, the out-patient list became a significant part of David Sharpe's work. Including those eighty patients who were admitted on the night of the fire, he saw 258 people who had suffered burns of one type or another. Some of them, particularly those with hand burns, might be seen at intervals for up to two years. "After about six months," David told me, "I probably wasn't doing more than one minor adjustment to a scar a week." Once again, although he can say, "We got rid of most of the deformities and problems right at the beginning", he cannot allow what ought to be a justifiable source of pride to go without adding the single word "surprisingly". It is almost as though it was nothing to do with him at all.

During those first weeks after the fire St Luke's had a number of visitors, including members of the Press, the Prime Minister, at different times virtually the whole of the Bradford City squad and, as has already been mentioned, one Robert Maxwell. Mr

Maxwell recovered from Dave Hustler's wicked sense of humour easily enough to ask if there was anything the hospital wanted. Dave Hustler himself recalled that special beds and left-handed surgical instruments soon appeared. But David Sharpe told me of another donation Mr Maxwell made, which was to endure for considerably longer.

Back in 1985 one or two people in Bradford, including Anthony Roberts, were volunteering to do some research into burns treatment. They were not being paid for their research work and there was no formal research unit. When David Sharpe heard Robert Maxwell ask if there was anything needed, he was bold enough to say that some money for a research unit and a fellowship would be very welcome. Robert Maxwell, never one to be affronted by a spot of boldness, donated £200,000 to help set up a research unit. Some further funds were allocated from the Disaster Fund administered by Roger Suddards and that gave an embryo investment from which it was possible to advertise for a paid post, initially for one research fellow. Today the University of Bradford Plastic Surgery and Burns Research Unit, to give it its full title, has four research fellows, but still relies heavily on donations, including those buckets that are passed round Valley Parade at the end of each season.

Another slightly unusual source of income for the research unit was the device so successful in restricting Dave Hustler's movements in the days following his own plastic surgery. David Sharpe himself had designed the Bradford Sling some time before the Valley Parade fire. This was not his only piece of design work and in 1988 he received both the British Design Award and the Prince of Wales Award for Innovation and Production. The uses of the Bradford Sling are not confined to burns surgery - I recently came across someone who had been put into a Bradford Sling after orthopaedic surgery following a serious traffic accident - but it is particularly effective where any elevation is needed. Dave Hustler's hands needed just that. Having designed the Bradford Sling, David Sharpe "didn't want the hassle of getting into manufacturing". Bradford University has its own company, Ventures and Consultancy Bradford, which is specifically aimed at making practical use of the university's work. VCB manufactures the Bradford Sling to David Sharpe's design and the royalties from its sale to hospitals throughout the country are given to the research unit.

What David Sharpe realised in 1985 was that the next generation of plastic surgeons, those who were just beginning to gain some practical experience, would progress more quickly up their professional ladder with a research degree. He also saw that this would allow the new research unit to attract committed and bright research fellows, who would want to produce some quality work in no more than two years. As he said to me, "This was not a job for life." The results have been at least as good as he could have expected, possibly better. The unit continues to attract highly-motivated research fellows who have produced papers adding to the world body of knowledge on subjects including scarring and tissue healing.

In keeping with the tradition of making the university's work of practical significance, the research unit's efforts have over the years produced a number of benefits for patients in Bradford and much further afield. One example David was able to give me involved work on scarring Asian children's burns. Just as he and his colleagues had to make decisions on the best way to treat the fire victims, so the researchers were able to show that on balance with certain types of burns the more conservative approach produced less scarring in these children. Work on tissue expansion has produced much better results after mastectomies and with burnt scalps. Other research has brought about improvements in the extent to which scar tissue contracts and current work includes the prospect of using hair follicles as skin substitutes. (Those of us who thought that might have something to do with a cure for baldness need not get excited - it's totally different, I'm afraid.) Bradford can be proud of having one of the bigger research units in the country and of taking its expertise into almost every other country in the world.

I interviewed David Sharpe in a small room at the Bradford Royal Infirmary during his morning theatre list. I was lucky that one of his patients had been delayed on the ward and that left him with a bit more time to talk to me. Eventually, like all good things, my chance to listen to this highly-skilled man came to an end. He was required back in theatre. But before he had to leave he told me one last thing about the treatment of the 258 people he saw back in 1985. What he told me was, in truth, more to do with the man who treated them, although I'm perfectly sure he didn't intend it that way. Having told me how most of the problems were faced and resolved in the early weeks, he finished by saying that this "was not a credit to us, but the way it went". I may not be the best qualified person to challenge David Sharpe's medical opinions, but I'm prepared to say that I think on this one occasion he's wrong. It seems to me and to those I've spoken to who were treated by that medical team back in 1985 that the results are truly a credit to them.

FOURTEEN

It was inevitable that a disaster on this scale, so graphically and instantaneously pictured and described by the Yorkshire Television cameras and John Helm, would bring about responses of all kinds. Even so, the extreme nature of some of those reactions could not have been quite so predictable. Once more we have to remind ourselves of the culture of the times, of the light in which football was predominantly cast in the mid-1980s. In those days the word most commonly added to any mention of football was "hooligan". It is easy to see how, in that context, the Press could be almost expected to run stories about how the fire at Valley Parade was started by some malicious or at best reckless act of a mindless yob. Matters were not helped by the death of a young supporter after a riot at Birmingham City's ground on the very same afternoon, a different kind of tragedy, but one made all the more uncomfortable by the undeniable fact that the visiting supporters that day in Birmingham were from Leeds, a city just 10 miles away from Bradford. Those who had an interest in claiming hooliganism as the cause of the Valley Parade fire were given one more round of ammunition to fire.

In the three weeks before Mr Justice Popplewell could even begin the public phase of his enquiry, still more football fans had died at a match in Belgium. Like the flames engulfing the stand at Valley Parade, the Juventus supporters being crushed at the Heysel Stadium were also on national television live in this country and this time across the rest of Europe as well. This was, after all, the final of the most important club competition in Europe and Juventus' opponents that night were an English club, Liverpool. It took no time at all for Bradford, Birmingham and Heysel to be joined together parrot-fashion as though they were all incidents of the same ugly phenomenon. That they were different, that Bradford at least was nothing to do with hooliganism, was something that the local community in the city wanted to make plain. That Bradford and Heysel have now gone down in football history and have since been joined inextricably, it often seems, with Hillsborough merely shows how a populist version of the truth can hold sway over the real version.

The Prime Minister in 1985 was, of course, Mrs Thatcher. She was not exactly noted for her love of football, either as a game or as an industry. Still less was she prepared to tolerate hooliganism, wherever it raised its ugly head. Her government was to introduce legislation for football membership schemes and to create criminal offences and penalties which applied only to acts committed in football grounds and not, for example, in rugby or cricket grounds. It was politically acceptable to dub our national game a national disgrace, for the very reason that it was indeed our national game. Some of England's club sides had been extremely successful in European competitions in recent years and accordingly English football attracted so much worldwide media attention. Throughout Europe football hooliganism had even become known as "The English Disease". How ironic, then, that "The English Disease" was still the description given to the rioting in Italy which brought about the abandonment of a game between two teams from Milan in 2005, by which time that sort of violence and large-scale disorder was practically unknown inside English stadia. And yet the very same Mrs Thatcher, perhaps better able than some to distinguish a true tragedy from the many surrounding incidents of hooliganism, was among the first to send her condolences to the families of victims and paid a famously long and genuinely sympathetic visit to the hospital where many were being treated.

In the city itself there were quite naturally fears that Bradford would be in the public eye for all the wrong reasons, for being the place where an old stand, in a state of acknowledged disrepair, had brought about the deaths of 56 innocent people. The city's response to these fears was to galvanise itself and its citizens to support the victims and their families. Val Walsh recalls, "I think to be fair you got cocooned in the community kind of spirit. People were so wonderful. The people of Bradford were so wonderful and I would have to say of all faiths, and that did give you some kind of glow that everybody was with you and it seemed more tragic and sad than blaming." Those who had no great affection for football and never went to matches still did not hesitate to involve themselves in a wide range of community projects. This was primarily a human tragedy in their eyes, even if so many of the victims also saw it as a football tragedy.

The City Council, under the direction of the Chief Executive, Gordon Moore, made its own contribution towards alleviating the immense distress suffered by so many of its citizens. Muriel Hainsworth, for example, having finished her voluntary stint at the Bradford Royal Infirmary on the night of the fire, then joined others in manning a special helpline set up by the City Council's Social Services Department to assist victims, family and those indirectly affected by the tragedy. For three weeks she and her colleagues listened to anyone who wanted to talk to them about how the fire had affected them. Some, it seems, quite literally just wanted to have someone to talk to for a few minutes. That one conversation was all they sought. Others were clearly in need of much more and those who took such calls would refer the callers to counsellors or other agencies that might be able to provide longer-term support.

The City of Bradford was also supported from a rather unusual source. Because the game had been intended to be a celebration of the team's success, the Lord Mayor of the City was in attendance. He was accompanied by a civic party from Hamm, Bradford's twin town in Germany. One member of that civic party was Joyce Reisner. She had grown up in Wilsden, a few miles to the northwest of the Bradford city centre. As a schoolgirl she had gone to Hamm on an exchange visit and there she had met Joachim Reisner, whom she later married. Joachim was an artist. Among his varying talents was a gift for sculpture. Joyce and the other civic guests were getting ready to leave the stand for half-time refreshments when the first flames emerged from Block G. Although they were all guided out of the ground uninjured, the images of what Joyce saw that afternoon went back to Germany with her. The people of Hamm decided to provide a memorial of the tragedy for the citizens of Bradford. Joachim Reisner was commissioned to fashion the gift that now stands outside City Hall in Bradford.

The sculpture stands, quite deliberately, just four feet high, so that children can read the names engraved in it and understand its significance. It depicts three bronze figures moving in a broken circle. These figures and the base of the sculpture are covered in the names of the 56 people who lost their lives as a result of the fire. The broken circle represents the ravaged stadium. The figures symbolise both the divide between life and death and those who reached out, both physically and spiritually, to rescue those in need of help. There are other memorials, not least that by the main entrance to the new stand at Valley Parade, which bear the names of the dead, but none does so quite as poignantly as this memorial. As Joachim Reisner said, "As I cast each letter of each name, I began to realise how enormous had been the damage done by the fire. In some cases the same surname occurred again and again. It was then that I knew how cruel the tragedy had been for those left behind." The citizens of Hamm provided a permanent and eloquent reminder of the effects of the fire. The citizens of Bradford walk past it in their thousands every day and every day some of them pause for a moment to remember.

One of the most obvious manifestations of the community spirit Val Walsh describes was the fund established immediately after the fire and overseen by local solicitor Roger Suddards. There had been other funds set up to support those who had suffered in other disasters. The way these funds had operated, and especially the manner in which money had been disbursed, did not always meet with popular approval. It is, therefore, a matter of some pride that Mr Suddards not only took time to examine how the management of these other funds had been conducted, but that he acquired a reputation based on his work in Bradford, which resulted in many others coming to him for advice. In particular he was consulted by those administering the funds for the King's Cross Fire and the Zeebrugge ferry disaster.

Contributions to the fund came from all over the world. While some donations came from more local sources, such as the City Council, the County Council and the Bradford-based supermarket chain Morrison's, others came from much further afield. Pennine Radio may have been very much a Bradford station, but the emotional description of the fire from its reporter Tony Delahunty was broadcast on Radio Eye, a radio station in Auckland, New Zealand. Donations to the disaster fund were made by listeners to Radio Eye before they had even seen the television footage which so graphically showed the devastation at Valley Parade.

At the time of the disaster the most successful team in England for some seasons had been Liverpool. Their fans had long since "borrowed" a song from the Rodgers and Hammerstein musical *Carousel* as the club anthem. To this day they sing *You'll never walk alone* before home matches. One Liverpudlian singer, Gerry Marsden (once of Gerry and the Pacemakers and *Ferry cross the Mersey*) came up with the idea of producing football's best known anthem as a record, with a B side containing messages of goodwill from celebrities including Paul McCartney. Sales of the record made a significant contribution to the amount raised. Perhaps Roger Suddards' best testimonial is that the almost £5million raised for the victims of the fire, itself evidence of the community spirit the disaster engendered, was distributed among the families of the injured and bereaved with hardly a single grouse. And that, given a combination of Yorkshiremen and money, is quite some achievement!

Bradford City Football Club had to make a number of momentous decisions in the aftermath of the fire. The most immediate concern was very personal. The club wanted to do whatever it could for the victims and their families without intruding into their private grief. Although at least one member of the club attended each funeral, the presence of the representative was kept low-key. Looking further ahead, the club had to face up to its liability in law. David Hall, for all his naturally very personal feelings about the fire, was still able to see the insurance position from his own professional standpoint. "A lot of people made claims against the club and its public liability insurance for their injuries and for the death of loved ones. I didn't because I thought that the club was already in enough trouble. If the combined actions of people exhausted the insurance money, which I understand being in the insurance industry, then that increased the chance that the club could have been made bankrupt and gone out of business." While David recognised that the law might not have put much of a financial value on his own father's life, he also readily accepted that some of those who had died or been seriously injured were breadwinners for families with children. "I fully understand why in those circumstances, if legal liability exists, a claim rightfully needs to be made." Perhaps the football club had limited choices, but it quickly admitted its liability through its insurers.

Another big decision for the club concerned the ruined stand and the crumbling terraces. There was quite simply no prospect of making Valley Parade fit for use by the start of the new season. As it turned out, City were to play their home games in the 1985-6 season and for the first half of the next season at Leeds United's Elland Road ground, at Huddersfield Town's Leeds Road ground and at the home of Bradford Northern Rugby League Club (as they then were) at Odsal Stadium. For some months the football club, the council and the rugby club considered the possibility of redeveloping Odsal into a stadium to be shared by the two Bradford teams. Odsal had once held a rugby league Challenge Cup Final replay with so many in attendance that they gave up counting at 100,000. Odsal had always been capable of being made into the "Wembley of the North", if only there had been the money. Valley

Parade was situated in an area where such a massive development, the creation of a 50,000 capacity stadium, was out of the question. It must have been a great temptation to leave behind the ruins and to build afresh.

If that was indeed a real temptation, it didn't survive many months. City's supporters were not now going to leave behind the ground where their team had played since its very first game over 80 years earlier and, most importantly of all, the ground where those supporters had died. I suspect that, whatever the financial problems and advantages of one choice over another might have been, they were never going to overcome the very clearly expressed wishes of those who remained faithful to the team. The heart was always going to rule the head. Valley Parade was going to have to be rebuilt and the new stand would have to be one where the fans could say with the utmost confidence, "It can't happen here again."

A new stand was built on the site of the burnt-out construction. Concrete and steel replaced the old wooden structure. There were more seats in the taller stand and the roof didn't leak! The Kop was re-terraced, the crumbling concrete replaced, new barriers put in and, for the first time in its history, the Kop had a roof. By December 1986 an England XI was playing the first match at the new Valley Parade and on 26th December 14,502 fans saw the first league game to be played in front of the new structure. With customary contrariness, City managed to lose 1-0 to Derby County! Much was to happen to that new stand and the ground as a whole in the next 15 years. Yet another football disaster, at Hillsborough in 1989, was to lead to yet another Inquiry, which produced a report recommending, among many other things, all-seater stadia. This time at least that aspect of the report wasn't ignored. Despite a reversal or two on the way, City were to make their way into the big league, The Premiership, in 1999 and the ground was to be further redeveloped beyond the wildest dreams of those who were in that old wooden stand. Today's all seater capacity of over 25,000 and the modern facilities for both corporate and full-time fans dwarf anything that ever existed on the site. But those developments, their consequences in financial terms and the ups and downs of one special football club around the turn of the millennium is another story for another place.

The important reactions to the disaster, both in the short and the longer term, come from those most closely involved in that dreadful day. Take, for example, Sue and Robert Hamilton. They were later to move house to live in Bradford, thus almost compelling Sue to share her football favours between Liverpool and Bradford City (I wouldn't have liked to try to work out what was happening in her head on that entirely improbable day in May 2000 when Bradford City had to defeat Liverpool to avoid being relegated from the Premiership and Liverpool had to win to secure a place in the European Champions League!). They had no hesitation in buying season tickets for seats in the new stand situated within a few feet of the very seat Robert had occupied back in 1985.

And Sue's ubiquitous transistor radio was to be the source of an almost equally disastrous alarm for her family in 1989. She and Robert were at Valley Parade when the radio told her of a "massive crush" and people being pushed forward in a cup semi-final between Liverpool and Nottingham Forest at Sheffield Wednesday's Hillsborough ground. This time, with her husband safely in the seat next to her,

Sue's concern was for her father. She knew he had managed to get a ticket for the semi-final and would be among the Liverpool fans. At first all that was plain from the radio was that the injured were from among the Liverpool rather than the Nottingham Forest supporters. Next came the news that there were probably fatalities. It was happening all over again for Sue. She was fairly confident that her father had a ticket for the seated area side-on to the pitch. For some time it was not obvious where the injured were coming from, although crushing seemed unlikely from a seated area. Eventually the Leppings Lane end of the ground was mentioned and Sue "was fairly sure he wasn't there, although it must have been harrowing for him to watch what was going on. When he realised people had died and seen people on stretchers, it must have been terrible." Four years earlier she had known that Robert was in the blazing stand. This time she still couldn't rest until she had made another phone call to make sure her father was alive and well. I don't know if Sue is sufficiently superstitious to believe that these things come in threes. If she does believe that, it doesn't prevent her still being seen with Robert at Valley Parade and Anfield on a very regular basis.

Norman Hall's son and daughter, David and Val, while they went through different experiences on that fateful day, have remarkably similar reactions to the events. Val herself was unable to talk about the tragedy for a very long time. Now she says that even her immediate anger with the press for the intrusive pictures of her brother soon subsided, albeit perhaps as a result of the medication she was offered. But so far as concerns the fire itself, Val has never spent her time looking for someone to blame. She soon came to acknowledge that "there were so many things that were actually wrong" without there being "a single body to blame". Mostly because of the overwhelming response of the local community, Val's view from very soon after the disaster was that "it seemed more tragic and sad than blaming".

Although her father, brother and husband were all at different times regular attendees at Valley Parade, Val wasn't a football fan. You might have expected that the very last place she would go to in future years was the stand where her father died and her brother received such serious injuries. "I think the fire made you either love City or hate it and I think that's still true today, that some people can't go near and many people have said that to me, 'I don't know how you could go near.'" But she did go near. On the Monday after the fire she went with an aunt to take some flowers to the remains of the stand. Shortly afterwards she went to the multi-faith service held on the pitch once the worst of the burnt-out debris had been cleared from the site. She thinks that maybe it was easier for her to go to the ground because she hadn't been there on the day. When she went to that service, "The memories were there without a doubt and I don't think at that stage I would have chosen to sit in the new stand." But for one who "wasn't particularly interested in football", she was later to be converted by her family, not least her two daughters, and eventually succumbed to joining the ranks of the season-ticket-holders.

Twenty years on and now, as a Justice of the Peace, a highly-respected member of the local community for which she has so much praise, Val still describes herself, however, as "a more fearful person". Even though, as she readily acknowledges, she wasn't present in person, she has developed an increased awareness of fire. She's always the one who reads that notice on the inside of the hotel door, the notice that tells you what to do in case of fire and where the nearest emergency exit is. In her professional life she has even had cause to make a firm point with her managers about quick and easy means of escape from where she works. She remains impressed by the transparency of what was done in the immediate aftermath, confident in the improvements that have been made since the fire, but most of all, "Now I think it was sad. I don't think it would happen today and I think all you can do is think some good things came out of it."

Her brother still adopts a diffident approach to what he sees as his part in his father's death. Although David recognises his "sane moments", when he can, albeit briefly, accept that he did as much as he could possibly have done, the dominant theme is still one of guilt. He readily praises the "wonderful job" done that day by the police and fire services. Beyond that he says, "It would probably have been easy to blame the club, but it served no real purpose. It didn't really come into my feelings." Apart from those times when he still questions his own bravery, he still says, "I'm a firm believer in life that there's a lot of luck. Some you make for yourself, some just comes your way. Some luck's good and some luck's bad. It was bad luck for anybody to be at Bradford City that day, especially for those who were injured and those who died or the loved ones of those who were injured or were fatally injured." He has, he says, "come to terms with it".

David never thought twice about not going back to Valley Parade. His father had first taken him there as a boy of 5 or 6. "I wanted to be there in memory of my dad." Even for David, however, there are two matches that stick very plainly in his memory. The first was in 1996, when his beloved Bradford City went to Wembley and won promotion to what was then the second division of the Football League by beating Notts County in a promotion play-off match. Just like in 1985, City were to play in the top half of the football league structure and joy was unconfined. Well, almost unconfined. It should come as no great shock to know that in the midst of the celebrations, David's thoughts turned to his father and he shed a few tears.

The other match that David remembered was at Everton's Goodison Park ground, when City had reached the dizzy heights of the Premiership. Long before then the Valley Parade stadium had been further and better developed. Wooden stands at Valley Parade were a thing of the distant past. But not so at this established Premiership ground. At Goodison Park David found himself on the back row, right in the corner of the upper tier of the timber-built stand used to accommodate the visiting supporters. "Before the game started I had what I suppose I can only describe as a panic attack," he recalled. "I'd not had one before and not had one since. I was frightened, I guess because I couldn't see a way out if something went wrong. I was very close to leaving the ground before the game started. I managed to just about cope with my agitation." So far as Valley Parade is concerned, "Going back has never been a problem, but it was that day at Goodison Park for five or ten minutes." Maybe we all of us need that sign on the door just to let us know the way we can evacuate the stand in two-and-a-half minutes.

FIFTEEN

On Monday 13th May 1985 Mr Justice Popplewell was sitting in the High Court in London. He was, somewhat ironically, hearing a case which concerned the pension rights of a fireman. Through his clerk he was asked to contact a man called Tom Legg, the most senior civil servant at the Lord Chancellor's Department. He was "invited", which is a term used in those circles to mean "told", to conduct an Inquiry into the events at Valley Parade and at St Andrews, the two football grounds where spectators had died two days earlier. He had been chosen by the Lord Chancellor, with the blessing of the Lord Chief Justice and the additional recommendation of the Prime Minister. It is rather difficult to refuse an "invitation" of that sort. He went back into court that morning to encourage the advocates in the case listed before him to ensure that it was finished within the time estimate of one day. The case did finish within the day and he was then free to think about his new task.

Sir Oliver Popplewell was not especially familiar with football grounds. His sporting interests were widespread, but his first sport was cricket. His son was a professional cricketer, given the dubious privilege on a number of occasions of going in to bat for Somerset immediately after or even at the other end from one I. T. Botham. Sir Oliver himself, after retiring from the Bench, continued doing some adjudication work, not least when he heard appeals against disciplinary measures imposed on international cricketers. On that Monday back in 1985 he knew that he was going to have some catching up to do, including visiting football stadia and other sporting venues.

His task was made no easier by the conjunction of the two events into which he was to inquire. He immediately recognised that the issues of crowd safety from Valley Parade and crowd control from St Andrews were very different from each other and required two quite distinct approaches. Indeed, if you read the first report he produced in July 1985, you will see that it is in reality two completely separate reports, the first half dealing with Bradford, the second half with Birmingham. (Yes, I know there's an old football cliché in there, but I've tried hard to avoid it!)

Sir Oliver came to West Yorkshire on the next morning after his High Court case was completed. He had a number of objectives, including meeting the Press and those who had been involved directly in the disaster. His primary concern, however, was to see the ground and the remains of the stand for himself. When in 2003 he published a book entitled *Benchmark*, he devoted a chapter to the Inquiry. Interestingly, although the Inquiry was officially into *Crowd Safety and Control at Sports Grounds* and thus covered the events and issues at both grounds, Chapter 8 of *Benchmark* is simply called *Bradford*. The catching up began with something of a sudden start, as Sir Oliver relates in his book. "The sight of the burnt-out stadium was horrendous and more awful than anything I had ever seen. Flowers had already been laid along the embankment above the ground. But they did little to alleviate the distressing picture of a stadium in ruins. This visit so soon after the disaster had a very sobering effect. It was gradually borne in on me the enormity of the inquiry in which I was engaged."

To a large extent Sir Oliver was allowed to decide for himself what form the Inquiry should take. That part which dealt with events at Birmingham City's ground was conducted in private. So far as concerned Valley Parade, it very soon became obvious to Sir Oliver that a public inquiry, at least in part, was necessary "in order to establish precisely what had happened, to enable those who were aggrieved or grieving to express their views and to enable us to decide what if any improvements could be made in relation to crowd safety". The City Hall in Bradford was a natural choice of venue to allow those who were grieving to give their own evidence and hear others do the same. Two assessors were appointed by the Home Secretary to assist Sir Oliver. One was a Chief Constable and the other a recently retired Chief Fire Officer. Both of those emergency services, alongside a number of other public and private bodies, were likely to come under some scrutiny during any inquiry.

Sir Oliver himself was then given the opportunity of appointing Counsel to the Inquiry. He chose Mr Andrew Collins Q.C., now himself a High Court judge. Among his various tasks Mr Collins was responsible for going through the mass of evidence collected by the West Yorkshire Police. They had taken hundreds of statements from witnesses. Many of the witnesses had been in the stand during the fire. Others were experts in various fields. There were numerous photographs taken during and after the fire, some more official than others. There were the tapes from the Yorkshire Television cameras, complete with the time along the bottom, a silent but truly dramatic addition to the account of how quickly the blaze had spread. Mr Collins had to review this mountain of material to decide how much needed to be put before the Inquiry.

There was an early hearing on 23rd May. While the Inquiry was not established to apportion blame, it was perfectly plain that sooner or later there would be the likelihood of court proceedings which would need to apportion liability and that, when the time came, any evidence given at the Inquiry would be used in those proceedings. With that in mind it was apparent that the interested parties would wish to be represented at the Inquiry. One of the functions of that first hearing was to make the arrangements for such representation. As a result, on the first day proper of the Inquiry there would be no fewer than nine counsel present, including three Q.C.'s. Apart from the two counsel to the Inquiry, the other barristers were representing the County Council, the Chief Constable, the Police Federation, the football club and, through the Bradford Law Society, the victims and their families.

Once that preliminary hearing was finished Sir Oliver went to visit some of those in hospital. What he saw remained fresh in his mind at the time he wrote *Benchmark*. "I was astounded at their courage and fortitude, and indeed at the general reaction of the citizens of Bradford to the great disaster which had overwhelmed them. The grief and anxiety and anguish which the disaster caused cannot be overstated. But the citizens seemed to draw on an inner strength and rallied round." It is not often that a city is described in such generous terms by a High Court judge. Bradford may have been more deeply concerned with facing the effects of the disaster rather than making a good impression on Mr Justice Popplewell. Nonetheless, the city clearly did make an exceptionally good impression upon him.

Sir Oliver and his two assessors heard evidence for seven days. A number of misconceptions and rumours had to be corrected. Three of the more serious stories were that the fire was caused by a smoke bomb, that a significant contributory factor was paint stored under the seating and that all of the exit doors at the back of the stand had been locked. None of these turned out to be entirely true. There was no smoke bomb in that stand. There was no paint stored under the seats. While it was true that some doors were locked, they were mainly the doors outside the turnstiles. Other doors were capable of being used as a means of escape, although it has to be said that lifting a bolt or removing a bar was hardly the easiest means of opening a door in the midst of total blackness, dense smoke and some chaos.

The Inquiry's purpose was to discover, as far as was possible, what the cause of the fire was, how it had spread so quickly and with such devastation and what lessons could be learnt to avoid any future tragedy of this sort. One of the major findings to come out of the evidence was a history of poor maintenance of the ground. Two years earlier Bradford City had gone out of business. The company formed in 1908 had ceased to exist and a new company had taken over the running of the football club, complete with its few assets and its considerable liabilities. And yet it was almost as though anything that had happened before the formation of the 1983 company could be disregarded.

The Inquiry was told, for example, of a letter written to the 1908 company by the Health and Safety Executive on 22nd June 1981. The letter made reference to a document known as the *Green Guide*. This document, much amended since 1985, is still used to this day. It was first produced in 1976 and was a direct result of the Inquiry into the Ibrox disaster of 1971. The Safety of Sports Grounds Act 1975 introduced the *Green Guide* as a series of recommendations to prevent further tragedies at sports grounds. The letter from the HSE made reference to two points from the guide. The first was the recommended time within which a wooden stand should be evacuated. For the Valley Parade stand that time was two-and-a-half minutes. The fire of 11th May took a few seconds over four minutes to engulf the entire stand. The second point was a reference to stands which have voids under the seating area; "These voids can become the resting place for ....combustible materials which can be ignited, unnoticed, by a carelessly discarded cigarette end." That paragraph of the guide almost exactly foretold what the conclusion of the Inquiry would be.

Because Bradford City had for many years played in either the third or fourth divisions of the Football League, Valley Parade had not come within the full ambit of the 1975 Act. The 1981 letter was, then, at the most a shot across the bows and in reality an invitation to do nothing. There was no follow-up letter from the HSE and the 1908 club, for whatever reason, took no action in response to the letter. To have removed the litter from the voids would certainly have required a large number of the floorboards to be pulled up and replaced. If the original boarding had been re-used, the same gaps would have allowed more litter to fall into the void. If new boarding had been used, there would have been even more cost to the club. Neither option was taken up and the litter remained where it was, in the gaps between the boards of the stand. No one knew how long it might take to evacuate that stand when it was full. It hadn't been as full as it was on the fateful day more than once or twice in years. Nobody in any official position, inside or outside the club, thought to ask whether two-and-a-half minutes was a realistic time within which to evacuate 4,000 people of all ages and with varying mobility.

Although Valley Parade was not a designated ground for the purposes of the 1975 Act, the West Yorkshire Metropolitan County Council had experience of at least one such ground, the Elland Road home of Leeds United. With the benefit of that experience and in the ever-optimistic hope that City too might one day reach the higher divisions, the County Council wrote to the old club in August 1982. That letter offered the services of the Council's officers and their guidance, should it be necessary for any work to be undertaken to prepare for designation. Perhaps those then responsible for the club did not share the Council's optimism about City's promotion prospects. There was no record of any answer from the football club. The Council didn't send any follow-up letter and the club needed no guidance until the ground was about to be designated - immediately after City won the third division championship at the end of the 1984-5 season.

The new company formed in 1983 was, however, more willing to seek the advice and support of the County Council. The old stand roof had leaked for years. Virtually every summer several new squares of bitumen had been added to the patchwork. Much as the new board of directors wanted to improve the dilapidated stand, money was very much an object. The club hoped to persuade the Sports Ground Trust that it should provide a grant which would at least go some way towards the cost of a new roof. In order to make its case, the new board sought the help of the County Council. On 4th July 1984 an engineer from the Council inspected the stand. Within a fortnight the club had a letter from the Council which it was able to use to make a successful bid for funding from the Trust. By March 1985 the steel for the new roof had been ordered. Because such an operation required scaffolding to be erected on the playing surface, the contractors could not start until the season had ended. The work was due to begin on Monday 13th May, immediately after the last match of the season.

That same letter of 18th July 1984, which the club put to such a constructive use, contained other comments. During the engineer's inspection a "build-up of combustible materials in the voids beneath the seats" had been observed. As was later to be discovered, some of that material had been there for twenty years. This part of the letter repeated almost word for word what the HSE's letter from 1981 had told the old company; "A carelessly discarded cigarette could give rise to a fire risk." It even made reference to the evacuation time. But the letter was written in the context of what the Council's concerns would be if Valley Parade came to be designated under the 1975 Act. In July 1984 even the new board of directors apparently did not expect that the season about to begin would bring promotion and designation.

So pleased were the officials of the 1983 company with what they saw as the helpful parts of the letter, the comments which supported their bid for a grant, that they either overlooked or at the very least failed to take any significant action upon those other parts which gave the sadly prophetic warning of what could happen. Once more there was no follow-up letter from the Council. Further consideration of what work might be needed did not begin until promotion was almost assured. The club and the Council agreed to meet to examine what work would need to be done to ensure that the newly-designated ground could be granted a safety certificate. The date for their meeting was fixed for Wednesday 15th May 1985. By then the meeting wasn't needed.

Much as the evidence given at the Inquiry disclosed a history of what might at best be called inertia, this in itself was not a complete surprise. Only two years earlier the club had gone into liquidation with debts believed to be around £400,000, a very significant sum for a company of this size. There were plenty of other clubs, including teams like Middlesbrough, playing in higher divisions, who were or had recently been in severe financial difficulties. Money was in short supply and safety considerations would often be well down the list of priorities, even in the days long before players' wages would eat up such a high proportion of a club's income. Anyone who had been in Valley Parade and especially in the stand would know how few improvements had been made over the years.

If a history of poor maintenance and unexceptional safety standards was to be expected from lower division clubs in financial difficulties, what was more surprising was the stance which the club took at the Inquiry. Stafford Heginbotham had been a director and, indeed, chairman of the old 1908 club, although he had had no links with the club between 1973 and 1983. He had played his part in forming the new company, ensuring the survival of the football club and finding a manager and team capable of bringing success after so many years spent in the lower divisions. Like any "saviour" of the local football club, especially when it becomes successful, he enjoyed something of a cult status in the city. It was commonly believed, for example, that the City Gent, one of the club's mascots, surviving in a very human form to this day, was originally modelled on Stafford Heginbotham when he was Chairman in the 1960s and 70s. Certainly the original cartoon figure of the man in the claret and amber kit, but wearing a bowler hat and carrying a black briefcase and umbrella, had the rather rotund characteristics which Stafford Heginbotham fought successfully to lose in his first spell as Chairman. Reading his evidence to the Inquiry, there is more than a hint of surprise when he explains that he himself mixed some of the concrete for The Paddock and the base of the lower seats in 1967. It was his way of losing weight and, at the same time, bringing about some improvements in the stand. Picture any current football club Chairman you might think of and try to imagine him or her mixing concrete! How the slimmer Stafford Heginbotham presented himself to the Inquiry certainly impressed Mr Justice Popplewell.

After the Inquiry at a hearing in the High Court before Mr Justice Cantley, liability was apportioned between a number of parties, including the football club. That is lawyer-speak for saying the judge decided who was to blame and how much each of them had to pay. But at the Inquiry "blame" was not the central issue. Indeed, listening to those involved and reading about the events of the time, there is a stark contrast between the responses to the Valley Parade fire and reactions to other disasters, be they football-related or not. Perhaps it is enough of an explanation simply to say that in the intervening years we have become more of a litigious society, more likely to go to court to establish who is to blame and, sometimes it seems more importantly, who will have to pay. With that in mind, the insurance companies and their lawyers often start by advising their clients to say nothing that might amount to an admission of liability. The Inquiry at Bradford took a very different turn.

We shall never know what advice the club was given by its insurers and lawyers, but we do know what its Chairman said in public before a High

Court judge. The first part of his statement might sound like the excuses. He reminded everyone that he had not been involved with the club for the ten-year period immediately before he had helped form the new company and pointed out that "very little work had been done in the ten years I was away". He talked about the effort he and his fellow directors had put into that two-year period and about what they had achieved in that relatively short time. He emphasised the priority which the new board had given to the leaking roof. He even told the Inquiry that the entire stand was to be re-concreted and re-seated; "The timber seats were to be taken up." So far he sounded like any other businessman (or even politician) defending his track record. But then the tone of his evidence changed completely.

By 12th June 1985, the day when he gave his evidence to the Inquiry, Stafford Heginbotham had seen the devastation at Valley Parade many times. He had attended funerals and church services. He had visited the injured. The human tragedies were bound to affect what he said to the Inquiry. "My own personal feelings are one of deep regret and a great sorrow felt for the loved ones of the people who have died and the people who have been badly injured. I would also like to say that I have thought a thousand times since then what more could be done, or what ought to have been done in order that such a tragedy could not have occurred or hopefully will never occur again, and hopefully a number of things will come out of this Inquiry that will assist not only Bradford City in the future but any number of clubs who are in a similar position." The grammar would suggest that this was not a pre-prepared, still less a lawyer-prepared, statement. Perhaps it was just from the Chairman's heart.

Stafford Heginbotham accepted that he was responsible for the way the club was run, for all the people who were employed in the management and day-to-day tasks required to be carried out, and for those duties which were not carried out. "There are obviously things that could have been done on that day or before that day that would have helped the situation with the benefit of hindsight. I am prepared to say," he concluded, "there are a number of things we all wish had been done or had been thought of prior to this terrible tragedy." The cynic might well point out how easy it was for the chairman of a limited company to admit almost anything in the safe knowledge that his personal financial liability was, by the very nature of the company of which he was chairman, strictly limited. Stafford Heginbotham need not, even from this apparent position of safety, have said what he said. Whatever his financial position may have been, and no matter how apparently secure in that sense he could be portrayed, he must have known from his previous experience as Chairman in the late 1960s and early 1970s that, when things start to go wrong, whether it is the team's losing run or an increase in the price of admission, the first person the fans are going to want answers from is the Chairman. If anybody is going to be criticised, the Chairman is. If you take the glory of being the "saviour", you have to expect the blame.

When Stafford Heginbotham gave his evidence to the Inquiry, the city, the club, the fans and most of all the bereaved and injured were still coming to terms with what had happened just a month earlier. Perhaps the tragedy was uppermost in everyone's mind to such an extent that the lawyers' version of a sensible response from the Chairman was overtaken by the purely human response from the Chairman.

Whatever the reasons behind the Chairman's frankness, it brought this judgement from Sir Oliver Popplewell in *Benchmark*. "It was a brave and responsible attitude to what was not merely a public but also a private disaster for the club." Some club chairmen would not have survived such an admission. Stafford Heginbotham's personal standing, either among the club's fans or further afield, was unharmed by his "brave and responsible attitude".

Ultimately, of course, the Inquiry had to come to a finding on how the fire had started, why it had been so devastating and what could be done to prevent a recurrence. Mr Justice Popplewell and his two assessors wrote their report in two parts. An interim report was published as early as July 1985. Sir Oliver quite naturally believed that there should be some urgency in publishing the Inquiry's preliminary views on how such a devastating event could be avoided. Much of the task of deciding how the fire started and why it had such horrific consequences was made easier by the large measure of agreement in the evidence given to the Inquiry. It was possible to come to findings on these matters very quickly. The lengthier task, that of giving detailed recommendations for the better safety of sports grounds, was hampered by Sir Oliver's lack of direct knowledge of how such grounds, and in particular football grounds, functioned during games. The fire had happened on the last day of the season, and so Sir Oliver had to wait until August before he could begin the practical exercise of going to grounds on matchdays and gaining the first-hand experience he felt essential before finalising any safety recommendations. A second and final report was not issued, then, until early in 1986.

The two Popplewell reports make fascinating reading, especially for those of us who regularly attend football matches up and down the country and who have the great benefit of hindsight. Unlike Mr Justice Popplewell at the time when he was writing his reports, we know something of what happened at Hillsborough in 1989. As he was writing *Benchmark*, when he too could claim the same degree of hindsight as we can now, Sir Oliver could only say, "Sadly, it [our report] could not prevent further problems at football matches, and I watched the disaster at Hillsborough with sadness." Many of the findings and recommendations contained in the reports are more closely related to crowd control issues than to matters of crowd safety, but there is, inevitably, some degree of overlap, not least in the difficult issue of fencing.

At Valley Parade in 1985 there was, in fact, perimeter fencing along the entire front wall of the Kop and the Bradford End. It is, of course, right to say that even in those days there was practically nothing on either of those concrete terraces that could be set alight. Even so, there might be other reasons for needing to evacuate an area of that type very quickly. In the interim report, there is to be found this paragraph: "A number of witnesses pointed out that if there had been closed perimeter fences at Bradford, the casualties would have been on a substantially higher scale. That is undoubtedly true." By the time he wrote *Benchmark*, Sir Oliver felt able to say "Quite clearly the presence of fences at Bradford would have enormously increased the number of deaths."

That climb from the lowest terracing at the front of The Paddock up to and over the pitch wall was, in its own right, a factor in a small number of deaths that afternoon. Fencing on top of that would surely have been much more disastrous, both in making that climb impossible for even more spectators and as another reason in the mind of many not to go to the front of the stand, but to attempt the "virtually impossible" escape route at the back. As we shall see later, there is no perimeter fencing at Valley Parade today, although there was when the stadium was first re-built in 1986. Indeed many parts of today's ground have no fixed perimeter walls, let alone fencing on top of a wall. This single issue, however, was very much alive back in the mid-1980s and illustrated better than any other the sometimes almost irreconcilable conflict between crowd safety and crowd control.

So far as concerns the two basic questions to be answered, the report is very direct and to the point. "The answer to the question how the fire started is that it was due to the accidental lighting of debris below the floorboards in rows I or J between the seats 141 to 143." It should be noted that the word "accidental" is quite deliberately inserted into that short judgement. The fire was not started deliberately or recklessly. We don't even know and no one was too concerned to establish with any precision if the actions of one identifiable person brought about that accident. The fire started by accident and no more is to be said on that point.

"The answers to the question therefore why the fire started and caused casualties are that, firstly the stand was a wooden structure, with a void under the seats, in which debris could and did collect; and secondly that the available exits were insufficient to enable spectators safely to escape the devastating effects of the rapidly-spreading fire." Here there is a little more to be said. Wooden structures with voids beneath were not uncommon in sports grounds in the 1980s. They had been there for years without any fatalities. Some are still there to this day. I can think of quite a few football grounds where I've sat in such a stand in recent years. I even sat in one during the time I was doing the research for this book. I've chosen never to look beneath the seating area to see if I can spot any debris underneath. I would hope there would be none, but I wouldn't guarantee anything.

The fact that the Valley Parade stand and so many more were constructed of wood gave rise to two particular recommendations in the report. One was that new stands should not be constructed of combustible materials. Sir Oliver describes in *Benchmark* something of a conflict he had with representatives of the timber trade, who suggested that his recommendations might be harming their members' businesses. He recalls meeting them, listening to what they had to say and then asking the one question, "Are you saying that a concrete stand is more combustible than a wooden one?" He then recalls a long period of silence, which he plainly took to be the answer to his question.

The second recommendation was that in any existing stand made of combustible materials, smoking should be prohibited. Even so, Sir Oliver himself, near the end of the chapter in *Benchmark* which deals with the Inquiry, says "I was taken to a ground in the northeast recently (given the date of publication of the book, I take that to mean perhaps in 2001 or 2002) where I sat in a wooden stand some 70 or 80 yards long. I was horrified to see that the stewards were smoking throughout the game, as were a number of spectators, even though the club had been warned that television cameras were to be introduced to film a programme about safety at football grounds. Lessons learnt from disasters seldom last long." I'm sure the club in question would have some explanation for this, which might include reference to the wood having been treated with some fire-retardant spray, but if Sir Oliver was not convinced by what he saw, why should the paying spectators believe they were sitting in a safe environment?

SIXTEEN

In a previous chapter I gave a description of what the Valley Parade ground, and in particular the old stand, looked like back in 1985. I said then how unrecognisably different it is today. There are many reasons for that complete makeover, not least Bradford City's rise to the Premiership for two seasons and the development associated with that higher status. After the Hillsborough Inquiry in 1989, all-seater stadia, especially in the higher divisions, became the accepted method of accommodating spectators. For a time there were complaints about the loss of atmosphere caused by the bulldozing of the old established terraces, but as time has gone by the Kop at Anfield and all the other famous standing areas seem to have created just as much atmosphere, even if it has meant in some grounds that "all-seater" has to be qualified by saying "for most of the time".

In the twenty years since the fire at Valley Parade, society has changed in so many ways. Football has gone through an utter transformation in the same time. While no one could claim that hooliganism has been eradicated to the extent that it can be regarded as a thing of the past, it is not the same problem that it was in the 1980s. The insides of football grounds are certainly safer in that respect. The financial changes in professional football have been on such a scale as would have frightened the directors of most clubs back in 1985. These changes have brought football ever further into the realms of business and at the same time have removed many of the essential features associated with a sport or a game. So big a business is football today that winning has assumed the most vital importance. The price of trying too hard to win and the cost of failure can be extinction for the club, as Bradford City can easily testify. Valley Parade, like all major grounds, has been developed to attract the corporate and more affluent supporter. Standing in the rain on a crumbling and weed-ridden terrace is no longer an option. If being seated means paying more, well that's just the way it has to be today. A new commercial reality is dawning, albeit in very different ways at different levels of the game.

Both the Popplewell Report on the events at Bradford and Birmingham and the Taylor Report on Hillsborough had their effects on the safety of football grounds. All those in and around football remember the Taylor recommendations for all-seater stadia, even though the report contained much else besides. That particular recommendation, like much of the Taylor report, was concerned with a mixture of crowd safety and crowd control. It is easier to control 5,000 fans each with his or her own seat than 5,000 fans standing in unmarked spaces and able to move about within a confined area of terracing. To the same extent, those 5,000 spectators in the seated area are safer, there being that much less risk of falling and crushing during the moments of highest excitement. There are, however, at almost all grounds changes which have been made since 1985 purely for safety reasons. Some of those changes would even go against the 1980s emphasis on crowd control.

I was very fortunate to be able to walk slowly round the west stand at Valley Parade, the stand built on the site of what was the only stand in 1985, while it was empty and while I was in the company of Chris Patzelt and Michael Chappell. Chris is the safety officer at Bradford City. Michael Chappell was head steward in 1985 and today is a customer care officer on matchdays. In 1985 there was no such post as safety officer. Today no club would be allowed to stay in business without one. Chris explained to me how he came to be appointed. There exists in each Local Authority area a body called the Safety Advisory Group. It is made up of officers (and sometimes elected members) of the Local Authority, the police, the fire service, the ambulance service and representatives from the football club. Each safety officer must satisfy the Safety Advisory Group of his competence to carry out the necessary duties. Otherwise the club breaches its safety certificate or plays behind closed doors.

Back in 1985, if there was a control room in the ground (and in those days there wasn't one at Valley Parade), it was very much the police control room. Particularly after Hillsborough, "everything turned on its head", as Chris Patzelt told me. While the police are still at the forefront of dealing with serious disorder, crime and the preservation of life and limb, the responsibility for safety is now very much with the club. There have been enough improvements in the hooligan problem to allow some games in the lower leagues to take place with minimal police presence, often nothing more than a handful of police "spotters", officers designated to look out for known troublemakers.

A football match is now seen as very much an event to be controlled by the organisation putting it on, in this case the football club, which controls the event via its safety officer and his team. On matchdays at Valley Parade it is a condition of the safety certificate that Chris Patzelt or his deputy is in the control room at least one hour before the turnstiles are opened and that he remain there until the last spectator has left. He will be joined there by

CCTV and radio operators, the senior police officer on duty in the ground, the police liaison officer and a representative of the ambulance service.

While on the subject of medical matters, Chris told me about the crowd doctor. The match day programme lists the club officials and includes the club doctor. He is, however, not the crowd doctor. The club doctor's primary duty is to the players. A quite distinct and separate duty is owed to the crowd. So, in addition to having a doctor present whose sole concern is for any casualty in the crowd, the club is required to have a qualified first-aider for every anticipated 1,000 spectators and an ambulance and paramedic crew for every crowd expected to exceed 5,000. Above that figure the required medical presence rises. Recalling his twenty years experience in football safety and the three people who survived heart attacks within the grounds for which he was responsible, Chris has a little smile when he assures me that a sporting venue is as good a place as most to be taken ill.

The more obvious safety features at Valley Parade immediately reflect the answers given in the Popplewell report to the central questions. The west stand is constructed of concrete and steel, with not a plank of wood in sight. Perhaps the timber industry has forgiven Mr Justice Popplewell for depriving it of one source of employment. There are no gaps in the flooring beneath the seats, so there is nowhere for the litter to collect, dry out and become ripe for ignition by a discarded cigarette. Such litter as there is drops on to the concrete structure and remains there only as long as it takes for the stand to be swept on the morning after a match. The seats are of the plastic tip-up variety so common at football grounds today. They may smoke, smoulder and melt, but they don't burn like those old wooden seats did.

And there is not a wooden beam or a single patch of asphalt to be seen in the roof, now constructed on a steel frame with metal cladding.

The other central deficiency identified by the Inquiry was that the available exits were insufficient to allow prompt evacuation. One of the ironies of that finding is that the evacuation time in 1985, two-and-a-half minutes to empty a stand capable of holding 4,000 people, has now become eight minutes for a stand holding more than double that number. The main reason behind this apparent relaxation is to be found in the non-combustible materials used in the new stand. The fire in 1985 took just four minutes to consume the entire length of the stand. In the event of fire today, such a rapid spread would be impossible. The stand and the ground as a whole could, however, still be evacuated for reasons other than fire and the eight-minute maximum still applies.

One of the recommendations in the Taylor Report, following on from all-seater stadia, was that no spectator should be more than 14 seats from the nearest gangway. Now you know why there are so many blocks of just 28 seats and not, say, 30 seats to a block. The gangways are of a standard width and stewards make a special point of keeping them unobstructed. Exits are clearly marked by the familiar green sign of the running man and the arrow pointing to the doorway. The whole process of getting people out of and away from the ground is treated, so Chris told me, like liquid in a vessel. Each stage, be it a gangway, an internal concourse or an exit into the street, has to be wider and larger than the previous stage, to avoid any bottlenecks and to allow for free flow. Calculations demonstrating how many people can be evacuated within a given time are even done on the basis that one in every five exits will be out of use by reason of whatever the emergency is that has brought about the need to evacuate.

On the day of the fire the best exit route, and the one eventually used by most of those who escaped, was on to the pitch. That climb over the pitch wall proved difficult at best, fatal at worst. Today that presents no problem. The west stand does have a wall at the front, but at the foot of each gangway the wall has an opening of the same width as the gangway itself. On two other sides of the ground there is no solid wall at all. The pitch is protected by nothing more than advertising boards, constructed like packaging for enormous bars of that triangular Swiss chocolate and light enough for the stewards to remove or overturn them easily in the event of any emergency. It is now clearly recognised that any evacuation arising from an emergency at the back of a stand may well require the spectators to leave by the front and on to the pitch. Perimeter fencing does not figure as a crowd control measure any longer - at least not unless or until the hooligan problem once more takes precedence over safety concerns.

One of the other problems in 1985 was that some of the exit doors were locked. Those immediately outside turnstiles could hardly be called exit doors. Even if those doors had been unlocked, there would still have been no way out past the floor to ceiling turnstiles that turned only to allow entry. But other doors, some of which were capable of being used as exit routes, were indeed locked. The keys for those doors were with stewards who were not in the immediate area. Today there is a steward allocated to each set of exit doors (the modern doors usually come in groups of four to allow a wider opening) and each steward has a set of keys and telephone contact with the control room. The 1985 "payment" to stewards, free entry to watch a football match, is no longer available to those stewards who remain throughout the game stationed at the exit doors, a position from where they have no view of the pitch. The much amended *Green Guide* also requires stewards for gangways and any other strategic position for evacuation. The total number of stewards at any game varies according to the anticipated attendance. There is a minimum figure of 1 steward for each 250 spectators, but there are always more stewards than that minimum figure would require.

There is still one startling reminder of how, even in a modern concrete and steel structure, a fire can start. The football fan is well known for his love of half-time refreshment. It may be prawn sandwiches in the corporate boxes, but for the average fan it will still be tea, coffee or maybe even a hot Bovril. There are those who famously eat all the pies - or burgers or chips or anything else the caterers might serve. The refreshment kiosk in the west stand main concourse is underneath the seats. Perhaps it goes without saying that it uses gas or electricity to cook the burgers, fry the chips and boil the water. But once you put such a source of heat underneath the seating area, you get something that bears quite a striking resemblance to what happened in 1985. Most grounds have their refreshment facilities under some seating area and the risk has to be dealt with. The risk is, of course, considerably less when the structure above the refreshment kiosk is made of concrete and steel. Even so, the kiosk in the west stand has steel shutters linked to the fire alarm system. They come down automatically if the alarm is raised and provide a screen against any fire spreading beyond the kiosk for up to half an hour. This has two safety features. The first and most obvious is that it stops the spread of any fire into other areas of the concourse, allowing the escaping fans the maximum space. The second and slightly less obvious result is that it prevents a repetition of that young man back in 1985 telling his grandfather, now that he's finally reached the front of the queue, he won't be leaving until he's been served. As the shutters come down, the staff won't be able to serve him or any of the others in the queue and the delay in getting them all out of the stadium will be that much less.

As one final illustration of the different emphasis put on safety since 1985, look at the structure of the organisations concerned with sports grounds and safety. Chris Patzelt, as the safety officer at Valley Parade, was appointed by the club and needed the approval of the Safety Advisory Group. He is a member of the Football Safety Officers' Association, a national body which has now turned itself into a limited company and looks forward to extending its remit to other sports venues. It provides information for its members on a secure website to allow each of them to benefit from the knowledge of the others in their own planning before any match. The Safety Advisory Groups up and down the country are monitored by the Football Licensing Authority, which is funded by the Department for Culture, Media and Sport. That Authority aims to ensure that all spectators "are able to attend sports grounds in safety, comfort and security", to quote their mission statement. Although they have statutory powers, they rely on persuasion and advice to pursue their aims. None of this national structure had even been thought of in 1985.

The Football Licensing Authority believes that "true safety comes when those who are responsible understand and believe in it for themselves". There can be no doubt that Chris Patzelt understands what safety is all about. Equally he plainly believes in safety, so much so that he can persuade others of its importance. He persuaded me that Valley Parade could never see another fatal fire like 1985's. But he knows that there are other ways of causing a disaster. I hope he won't think me too cynical or pessimistic for believing that the ingenuity of man is complex enough for someone somewhere to do something, accidentally or deliberately, to beat even the most sophisticated of safety systems.

I don't go into that west stand very often these days. Maybe, after so many years in the same seat, I've just got used to watching games from a different spot in the ground. As I did my gentle tour through the empty stand, I could work out to within a seat or two where the fire started, where the old exits had been and a host of other details from nearly twenty years earlier. Of course I knew it couldn't happen again here - could it?

SEVENTEEN

In the earlier pages of this book you will have read about what happened before, during and after 11th May 1985 through the stories of all sorts of people who each witnessed some of the many different events of the time. You may have gathered that I have been a regular at Valley Parade for many years and you might guess that I am even more committed to my club as a result of what happened that day. What you may be unsure about is my involvement in the events. I've told the story from the points of view of as many others as I could fit into this book and I was going to leave it there. But by keeping quiet about myself I realise I'm at risk of cheating my reader - or at least those of you who don't know me. I've decided in these last few pages to tell the story from one more point of view - my own - not least because it helps a little to explain more clearly why I was so keen on preserving the memories from that day, sad as they may be. I didn't save any lives. I didn't pull one single person over that wall. I didn't heal anyone, mentally or physically. And I didn't have to go through that harrowing night wondering whether my family and close friends were still alive. That's why I wasn't going to put my story in. But I won't cheat. I shall admit at this late stage that I was in the stand and, even though it has none of the elements I've just listed, I shall give you the chance to read what happened to me. Or you could always choose to skip the last few pages of the book!

I'd better start by telling you about my relationship with one or two of the people from the earlier pages. Arnold Whitehead, then just short of his 65th birthday, is my father-in-law. And I'm pleased to say "is", because he's still in fine form at 85 years of age. We were sitting next to each other, as we had done at plenty of games, when the fire broke out. More of that at the appropriate time. Sitting on the other side of Arnold was my friend Robert Hamilton, he of the "virtually impossible" escape. Again, more of that later. I knew his wife, Sue, not least because I was best man at their wedding. Another wedding I went to was that of Chris and Val Walsh, although at the time they were friends of my then fiancée. You can imagine how we've become good friends in the intervening years.

If that sets the scene with some of the people I've known, the real scene will now have to speak for itself. You won't want me repeating how the stand was laid out, what it was built of and all that went with that description. Sufficient to say that I loved the old "Sopwith Camel", raindrops and all, but even I have to admit that the new ground is vastly superior in almost every respect. I shall try not to repeat too much of what's gone before, but you'll understand that there has to be a bit of an overlap. This, then, is what happened to the luckiest man in Valley Parade.

You could always get a seat in the stand, usually even at five to three just by paying on the day at the turnstile. Tickets bought in advance were a rare necessity. This game, however, was special. I'd been watching City for nearly 25 years and at last we'd won a trophy more important than the West Riding Cup. The ground and thus the stand was going to be a sell-out. We thought we'd better get some tickets. The three of us - Robert, Arnold and myself - all worked. Ann, my wife, was swiftly delegated to nip down to the ticket office during the week and get tickets for the three seats we always tried for, on the back row of Block F. That worked a treat and all was in hand for us to meet up at the game. Arnold and I would travel the few miles from his house in my car and Robert would come over from Manchester on the coach. We got there in good time and I brought Ann's camera to record the presentation of the trophies and the lap of honour before the match. It was one of those cameras that needed no particular skill, thankfully, and it would fit into the inside pocket of the shower-proof jacket required by the temperature. Before kick-off I took a few pictures of the celebratory scenes. They have no great artistic merit, but they survive to show what the view was like from the back row. It never occurred to me to use that camera at any time after the kick-off.

I have no recollection at all of the game, so good was it, until about 3.40. Sitting to my right, Arnold for some reason had put his hand down between his knees and, through the gap under the wooden seats, had felt an unusual warmth. Just to be sure he wasn't mistaken, he put his hand down again, turned to me and said, "It's getting a bit warm here." I then did much the same with an identical result. Around the same time just to our left and a few rows below us people were starting to leave their seats in a bit of a hurry. As a small space cleared, I could see just a wisp of light grey smoke, as if someone had set a waste bin on fire. As that space got larger and the smoke ever so slightly more widespread, Arnold turned one way to me and the other to Robert and said "I think we'd better get out of here." We were later to realise that, although we couldn't see any flames, the heat in the void beneath the seats was already advancing at some speed up the stand and towards the Bradford End.

We were sitting to the Kop side of the aisle that ran down the centre of Block F. I was nearest the Kop, Robert furthest away. On Arnold's suggestion we all rose together and made the short journey to that aisle and into the back corridor. Further along Block F at several games we'd seen this young lad, a teenager we guessed, who could walk only with the aid of crutches. I know now, of course, that that was Matthew Wildman. I'm fairly sure he was along that row that day. I know that, later on, the three of us wondered out loud to each other what had happened to him. I'm glad to say, thanks to Dave Hustler and another man, we were all wrong.

By the time I got into that back corridor, there were already plenty of others making their way towards the halfway line and away from the source of the smoke in Block G. The volume of grey smoke now seemed to be growing surprisingly quickly. Almost immediately I seemed to lose sight of and any other contact with Robert, although he could scarcely have been more than a couple of paces in front of me. In that mass evacuation a couple of paces could be the equivalent of quite a few people and several vital seconds. Arnold, I knew, was right at my side, literally shoulder to shoulder, save for the few inches difference in our height. We'd not been long in that corridor when the smoke began to get under my glasses. Bad as my eyesight was, I could see even less through the smoked-up lenses. Both Arnold and I removed our glasses, although we held them in very different grips.

Progress along the top corridor was very slow, somewhat pressured, but not what you could truly call panicky. And then came the moment that changed everything up there. Have you ever sat in bed reading, then turned the light out and tried to see anything at all around you in the darkened room? Maybe your eyes adjust after a few seconds and make out some shapes. But just for a few moments you can't see anything at all. That's just what happened in that top corridor, except that the few moments never came to an end. I quite literally couldn't see my hand in front of my face, let alone Arnold, Robert or anyone else, no matter how closely we were all squashed in together. What I now know is that this was the moment the smoke from the bitumen roof above us overtook us as the fire spread "as fast as a man could run". Only we weren't running. We were barely moving. And now I could sense the panic was setting in.

I could still feel Arnold's shoulder pressed against the upper part of my left arm, so I knew we two at least were still together and going the same way. Without saying anything, but knowing what I thought I knew of the stand, I was heading along the entire length of that walkway to the door at the far end, the door that led into the clubhouse, the door that was never locked and the door that led almost straight out into South Parade. At least that was the theory. I reckoned Arnold was the only person to my left. He, then, would be right against the wooden fence that formed the backrest for the top row of seats. We were as far away as it was possible to be on that corridor from the turnstiles and doors leading from and into South Parade. Anyway, I reckoned, the turnstiles would be no good because they turned the wrong way. There was no use trying to get out that way. The other doors had always seemed to be locked until what was commonly known as "three-quarter time". There was no point in trying them either. But it didn't matter because that end door, I was confident, would see us all to safety. There, then, was my version of logical reasoning in those few blacked-out moments.

You will observe straightaway that one possible means of escape hasn't even come into my thinking. Robert and I had been at school and university together, both winning prestigious awards to go to Oxford. In his interview he admitted not making the best decisions that afternoon, but, remember, he got out unscathed. This other brilliant lad here didn't even think to go down the stand and over the wall on to the pitch. Maybe I too was just another law-abiding citizen. Even they are allowed a bit of a trespass to save their lives. But it never entered my head - at least, not at that time. One thought and one thought only stayed with me - the door into the clubhouse and all would be well. Arnold, so far as I could feel, was right with me.

As I made my painfully slow progress along that jet black corridor, I could hear cries I would prefer to forget. I might prefer to forget them, but I don't. They were from some of those who were desperately trying to get through those turnstiles that turned the other way or those doors that were locked or bolted. Their cries merely confirmed in my mind that my route was the only safe way out of that smoke. If I'd known Glynn Leesing's view then about the "virtually impossible" escape, I would have struck out the "virtually", at least so far as concerned those doors on to South Parade. It was somewhere around here that, for a very fleeting moment, I thought about the toilets as an escape route. But I knew there was only one way in and out, back on to the top corridor, and I'd forgotten about the high windows. I'm not sure I'd have fancied my chances up there anyway, but it didn't matter because I dismissed the whole idea as soon as I thought about it. I never even tried to force my way across the walkway towards the toilet entrance and exit.

As I carried on with my slow journey in the blackness, I remember bumping into a barrier with my left thigh. There was some comfort in that, because it meant I'd reached halfway. The tubular barrier was where you queued for your cup of tea. Although progress had been very slow, there didn't seem to be anyone falling over, being trampled on or crushed. Even then I had time to remember Burnden Park and Ibrox, where people died from being crushed. Remaining upright was what mattered. Nobody that I knew of had ever been burnt at a football match.

I've no idea how long I'd been in that total blackness before I realised I was having problems breathing. I was 33 years old, strong and fairly fit, although I'd given up my regular football five years earlier when my knees wouldn't go back down to normal size for four days after a match. Looking back, I guess I'd have still had trouble breathing in that atmosphere if I'd been as fit as the players I'd just been watching. I know now, of course, that there was a fire below me, above me and ahead of me that was using up whatever oxygen it could get. The fire below me, in the seating area, was probably still behind me and must have been fighting the roof fire for the available oxygen supply. I don't know where I got it from, but I remembered something about air in a fire being better quality or easier to breath at lower levels. Having worked out that nobody was being trampled on, I thought I could take the chance of ducking down, bending my knees like Groucho Marx, and for a shuffle or two ("steps" would be an exaggeration) gulp in some cleaner air. I was beginning to think I wasn't going to make it to the safety of the clubhouse.

Twice I managed to breathe what seemed to me like cleaner, less smoke-logged air from about waist height or below. We didn't stop shuffling along and I made sure I retained my balance. There was something akin to drowning in this whole scenario, except that you didn't come up for air, you went down. As I was about to go under for a breath of air for the third time, it finally dawned on me that I really wasn't going to make it to the end of the corridor, even though I'd still no idea how far along I'd reached.

Somewhere in the utter blackness which had surrounded me for so long, I saw, quite literally, an opening, a shaft of light. Immediately I recognised it as the grey smoke that had filled up my glasses earlier on. Grey smoke that you could see into was a whole lot more appealing than black smoke that blinded and choked you. It was to my left and below me. It was somewhere in the direction of the pitch. Law-abiding thoughts had gone. Survival had taken over. I decided that I was going toward the grey smoke, out of the blackness, away from the clubhouse door and down from the top corridor. I remember very plainly making that decision up there on that walkway. I've no idea how I put it into practice, nor have I ever had.

The next thing I knew, I was facing that wall at the side of the pitch. It came most of the way up my six-foot frame and I needed a good swing of the legs sideways to get over it. As I made my attempt at gymnastics, a man to my right tried the very same manoeuvre at the very same moment, except that I swung my legs to my right and he swung his to his left. In the tiny gap between us a clash of legs was inevitable and neither of us made any progress. Without a word being spoken, we managed to work out the quickest rota you've ever seen. He swung first, I swung second and we both pulled ourselves over the wall on to the track. There was a policeman within feet of us, telling us to move away from the wall, get on to the grass and make room for anyone else behind us. I thought there must be at least one more person behind me, so I moved three or four paces forward, my spectacles still folded in my hand. I began to look sideways as I took those few steps, looking for Arnold, who must be the next one over. I couldn't see that section of the wall that I'd just staggered over, so I stopped and turned right round, about five yards on to the pitch, just outside the penalty area at the Bradford End.

I'd travelled probably three-quarters of the length of the stand and now, for the first time all afternoon, I saw a flame. I'd not seen one before. I'd seen wispy smoke, grey smoke, thicker grey smoke and I'd been engulfed by jet black smoke. But I'd not seen one single flame until now. And the first flame I saw was coming from right behind the wall that I'd just climbed over. That section of the stand, where I had been a few seconds earlier, was on fire from top to bottom. This wasn't a flame. It was an inferno. It was like working in a foundry, a job I'd done for a little while as a student. The only difference was that you didn't have to open a furnace door to be blasted by the heat. At Valley Parade the heat blasted you in the open air and at a distance of some yards. All this despite the fact that the flames were being blown away from you and into the remains of the stand. But the heat and all that went with it didn't register for a while. Only one thing registered with me. I couldn't see Arnold. But he'd been right behind me all the way. And he was thirty years older than me. And I'd only just got over that wall.

By now the police were moving those of us who were still anywhere near the wall further towards the middle of the pitch. I don't suppose the heat would have allowed me to stay there much longer in any event, but I was walking backwards, staring at the wall, the flames just beyond it all the way up to where the roof used to be. I was staring into the bottom part of the flames. No one was coming out.

But someone must come out and it would be Arnold. But no one did and slowly I edged into the middle of the pitch, just outside the penalty area. All those years I'd longed to be just there, on the edge of the box. And now the hallowed turf was just a piece of grass with hundreds of us milling about on it, bewildered, searching, pleading, not one of us dreaming of being there at that moment. There were only nightmares for us now - except these nightmares were really happening.

Once I knew for sure that no one else was coming out of those flames, I began my search of the pitch. I went up and down, in and out among so many others doing the same thing, looking for family and friends. Robert was going to be the easy one to spot - fairly tall and very red hair. I wasn't to know I was looking in totally the wrong place. Arnold was more difficult - somewhat shorter and I couldn't remember what he was wearing. Up and down the pitch three or four times, moving nearer to the Midland Road side and then back again as close to the stand as the police and the heat would allow, just to cover a slightly different patch of grass with each trek. But there was no Robert, no Arnold, nobody I recognised. And then the police started to move those of us still there off the pitch and into the Bradford End and out of the ground through a big wooden gate they'd managed to open. Another section of terracing to climb into - that's all there was at the Bradford End in those days - with the greatest reluctance. I was still looking backwards and around me at the diminishing numbers still on the pitch. There was no sign of anyone I knew. The young policeman was very good at ushering us out of the ground. Maybe my law-abiding nature had returned by then, because I didn't argue. I just paused long enough to ask if he knew whether everybody had got out. It may seem a silly question now, but I was just like everybody else. I didn't want to believe anyone could die at a football match. The young policeman didn't give me an answer. The look on his face, the movement of his shoulders and the drop of his head told me what I needed to know.

Outside, behind the Bradford End on the steep slope of Holywell Ash Lane that leads down to Midland Road, I had regained enough of my senses to work out a plan pretty quickly. Nobody coming out of the ground at that end was being allowed to go uphill, back towards the burning stand. At the bottom, at the corner of Midland Road, the ambulances were beginning to arrive. The Midland Road exits were at that corner and further along, in a straight line of vision. From that corner I could see both exits and everyone who came out. I could see the ambulances and I could snatch a quick look at the faces on the stretchers before they were put in and whisked away. None was Arnold. Certainly none was Robert. I looked at a lot of faces and I don't want to remember any of them.

I've no idea how many stretchers I looked at or how long I stuck with my plan. What I do remember is that the numbers leaving from the Midland Road exits dwindled and I thought I'd better try Plan B. The only trouble was I didn't have a Plan B! A little more thought told me that Arnold and I had come in my car. If he was anywhere, he would be near the car, which was parked up Queen's Road. There was only one way to and from there, so I couldn't miss him by taking a different route. I set off to run along Midland Road and turn right at the police station end, up Queen's Road to where I'd parked the car. It didn't take me too long to find out that I couldn't run. Although I didn't truly believe I was that unfit, I put it down to my lack of recent exercise and settled for walking as quickly as I could with the odd jog for short distances. Eventually enough of my brain began to function again for me to work out that lungs full of thick smoke are not ideal for a runner.

As you go along Queen's Road it drops for a while until it reaches the junction with Station Road to the right. Beyond there is the bridge over Canal Road and my car was parked on that bridge. Again the sightline is good. You could see the row of parked cars and the grass verge alongside them from some distance. I knew that Arnold couldn't get into the car, because I had the keys. I was looking for him standing by the car or leaning against the bridge parapet. I was looking and walking, but I wasn't finding. I kept walking nearer and nearer to the car and trying to think what to do next. As I approached the Station Road junction, I was within 50 yards or so of the car. I could see the car, but there was no sign of Arnold. I decided to turn round, go back on Midland Road and resume my gruesome ambulance-watching.

By now I was right on the junction with Station Road and about to turn round, when I saw a car, which had pulled out of the same line of parked cars where mine was. I didn't recognise the car or the driver, not even when it began the very slow turn round the sharp left-hand bend into Station Road, by now just a few feet in front of me. I was actually in the roadway, although not in front of the slowly moving car. The driver must have wondered what was going on when I jumped in front of his car. Maybe I didn't have all my faculties, but I must at least have cleaned my glasses, because I recognised the man in the front passenger seat of this unknown car. It was my father-in-law! The car stopped, I waved my arms like a mad thing, Arnold got out and

I almost lifted him off the ground as I hugged him. Looking back, I suspect something like 20 minutes had passed since I had last seen him, although it had seemed like forever. For most of that time I had feared the worst. I was so relieved I didn't even notice his injuries for long enough.

Arnold, as he was able to tell me over the following days and weeks, had decided to go down through the seats before he had reached the halfway line on that walk along the back corridor. For a lot of the time while I had been in the blackness, convinced he was right next to me, he was making his way over seats, down drops, being picked up at the bottom of the deepest drop, down into The Paddock, by an unknown man and finally being pulled over the pitch wall by John Hawley. It seems that he had left the ground by one of the Midland Road exits while I was still searching up and down the pitch. Somewhere along Midland Road he had come across Eric and Wendy Lee, old friends from a house they had lived in years before. I didn't know them at that time, although I knew Eric's brother Jack, and there is a distinct likeness. The car that I'd seen turning so slowly into Station Road was driven by Eric. They were taking Arnold home and Eric had to stop when this madman jumped in front of them with his arms in the air.

I have often reflected on the fact that, had I been a few seconds earlier or later at that junction, I would have missed Eric's car and gone back to the corner of Holywell Ash Lane and Midland Road to resume my ambulance-watching. I don't know how long I would have kept that up or how soon I would have gone back home to tell my wife and her mother what I feared. It didn't happen that way and once more I was so much luckier than so many who were still searching hours later.

I drove Arnold back to where Ann and I lived in Thackley, a journey of two or three miles from Valley Parade. There was no one at home, because our wives had gone out for the afternoon with our young son. Just as I turned into the driveway I noticed Martin Lawson washing his car in his own drive. Martin and Anne lived just two doors away. Martin had had his car radio on, had heard what was then being broadcast about the fire at Valley Parade and knew I was at the game. They both came round immediately to see if Arnold and I were injured and it was only then, when Anne expressed her concern about Arnold's head, that I realised for the first time that he had been burned. A damp cloth was found in the kitchen and Martin insisted on taking us both to the Wharfedale Hospital, reasoning that the main Bradford hospitals would already have enough to do. Anne waited at home for the return of the two wives, so that she could tell them that all was more or less well.

We hadn't gone very far in Martin's car when I saw Ann driving her mother and our son in the opposite direction, on her way home. I didn't know if they knew anything about what had happened and we were past each other before I could do or say anything. It turned out that Ann had turned on her car radio too, just to find out what the result from Valley Parade was. Instead of hearing a football result she heard Tony Delahunty's broadcast about "human torches" and people barely escaping with their lives from the stand in the vicinity of the press box. Ann had bought those three tickets. She knew where those seats were and how much further away from safety their occupants had been. For her the saving grace was how near she was to home when she switched on the radio. She had no more than two minutes to digest what she had heard before she saw my car in the driveway of our house. She knew then that at least one of us was safe. Courtesy of Anne Lawson's presence of mind in staying by our house, Ann and her mother soon knew the important parts of the story.

At this stage the missing link, if he will forgive me, was Robert. Neither Arnold nor I had seen him since those first few steps into the top corridor. My search of the pitch, the exit gates and the ambulances had proved fruitless. We'd heard nothing when Martin took us off to hospital. Ann can have been in the house for only a few minutes when the telephone rang. The caller was Robert, somewhere in the city centre with no clear idea how he'd got there. Ann was heading for the hospital, but had time to give Robert directions to our house. As we know Sue was also later to ring the same number from Liverpool and to receive the news that her husband was well. By not much after five o'clock our little group and their families had, at least by messages, been re-united and reassured.

Meanwhile, at Wharfedale Hospital Martin had stayed in the car to keep up with the radio news bulletins, while Arnold and I had registered with the nurse on reception and joined just one lady in the waiting area. She appeared to be with someone already being treated. Arnold's burns were to his scalp, the tops of his ears and the backs of his hands, just as David Sharpe might have predicted. I had a mild soreness to the top of my head, which was eventually treated as one of the less deep-seated burns, thanks mainly to the full head of hair I enjoyed in those days. While waiting for Arnold's turn, I said I was just going to nip out to the car park to ask Martin what the latest news was. The lady in the waiting room became very concerned about my intended departure, even though it was only a short distance to the car. Even my explanation that I was clearly third in a queue of three and not at all fearful of losing my place did not seem to placate her. It wasn't until I got back home and saw myself in the mirror for the first time that I appreciated why she was so concerned for me. The few bits of me that were visible, mainly my face and hands, were uniformly grey. In the mirror I saw a smoke-logged face. The lady in the waiting room, my guess is, suspected she was looking at a heart attack victim. If she remembers me, the smoke washed off.

The other thing I spotted for the first time back at home was a clue, indeed the only clue I've ever had, to my missing time, from making that decision at the top of the stand to vaulting over the pitch wall. I've never known how I got there or who, if anyone, may have helped me. But as I undressed for a shower to wash off the smoke, I saw my trousers had horizontal yellow lines across the front of both legs from just below the knees. I think the explanation is simple, that in that downward journey I was climbing over the backs of seats that were melting. I guess even at that end of the stand it was already pretty warm. I have to guess, too, that something fairly grim happened in that journey from the top corridor to the pitch wall. I'm told that the reason I can't remember anything about that time is because I have what the psychiatrists call a "dissociative disorder". In terms that I think I can understand, it means that my mind has spotted something that it doesn't want me to be able to remember, so it won't let me recall it. And that will very probably be permanent.

The rest of the story for me lasted another eight days. In that time I went back to work on the Monday morning, because that's what you do. One of the local reporters in Manchester wrote a story for the *Manchester Evening News*, where they managed to add twenty years to my age and to change my father-in-law's name to Harold. By Tuesday evening I was in tears, and all because of an item on the radio news that Notts County, who had been relegated on the same day that City had been promoted, were sending a donation to the disaster fund. On Wednesday morning I had to admit that I hadn't actually got any work done in the last two days and that I still had a talk to prepare for Friday and a training event for Saturday and Sunday. Philip Dodd, my then boss, was kindness itself and relieved me of those burdens. Instead I spent my Sunday afternoon giving a statement to a detective from Dewsbury. After three hours and thirteen pages of his handwriting, he felt obliged to say he had never taken any statement quite like it before.

And since I'm being totally honest, I have to admit that my story didn't last just another eight days. The nightmares lasted several months and the memories will last forever. In 1999 at Wolverhampton Wanderers' ground, City won promotion to the Premiership. It was to be their first season back in the top division since 1921 and it was going to be very much more lucrative than it had been 78 years earlier. My little team had made it into the Big Time, something I never thought I'd see. Those of us who were there were overwhelmed by the occasion. For me there was just one minute when, in the midst of the leaping about, the singing, the cheering and all the excitement, I just had to sit down. I couldn't help but remember those people who had died without seeing anything like this. I was soon back on my feet, cheering with the rest of the lads, just as I cheer as loudly as ever immediately after the little cry I have before the last match of the season, when we nearly always remember our dead. Four minutes has become a lifetime, I'm proud to say.

There, then, is my part in this story, for what it's worth. As I said at the start, I didn't do any of the things done by Glynn Leesing, Gill Page, John Hawley or Dave Hustler that afternoon. I wasn't with Muriel Hainsworth or Peter Jackson comforting the injured and their families that night. I didn't have to chase round hospitals and police stations all night like Chris Walsh and Teresa Hall. And I couldn't be part of David Sharpe's team in that following week. If you've read right up to here, don't try to remember my story. There are hundreds of others from that afternoon, lots very much like mine, that I haven't got room to tell. But do try to remember, at least once a year, some of those earlier stories. Whether we call what they did professionalism, skill or genuine bravery, those people deserve to be remembered. The most I can hope to do in this book is to preserve those memories.

POSTSCRIPT

The very last paragraph of that part of the Interim Report of the Popplewell Inquiry to address the events at Valley Parade sums up for me the most significant feature of 11th May 1985, a feature I have come across time and time again as I have worked on this book. I cannot improve on Sir Oliver Popplewell's words and so I end, with respect, by repeating them.

"Finally I cannot finish this section of the report without paying tribute to the enormous heroism shown by a very large number of people at Bradford. It would be invidious to single out any individual or group of individuals. They came from all walks of life. They all played their part in saving lives."